Learn To Cook And Eat The Mediterranean Way

Myla .Y Guerrero

Introduction

Embark on a culinary adventure with this book, a guide that invites you to savor the flavors of one of the world's most renowned and healthful diets. This book goes beyond recipes, offering a comprehensive exploration of the Mediterranean diet, its benefits, components, weight-loss potential, and practical tips for seamless integration into your lifestyle.

Delve into the heart of the Mediterranean diet, understanding its essence and the cultural roots that have made it a symbol of healthful and delectable living. Explore the multitude of health benefits it offers, from heart health to overall well-being, uncovering the secrets behind its reputation as a lifestyle that promotes longevity.

Immerse yourself in the primary components of the Mediterranean diet, from wholesome grains and heart-healthy fats to an abundance of fresh fruits and vegetables, gaining a deeper understanding of its nutritional foundation. Navigate through common myths and facts surrounding the Mediterranean diet, dispelling misconceptions and providing clarity on how this culinary approach can enhance your health.

Discover how the Mediterranean diet can be a delicious and effective strategy for weight loss, offering a sustainable and enjoyable way to achieve and maintain a healthy weight. Receive practical guidance on how to get started, making the transition seamless and enjoyable for individuals at any level of culinary expertise.

Equip yourself with valuable tips for navigating grocery stores and restaurants, ensuring that the Mediterranean diet becomes a practical and realistic part of your daily life. Embark on a week-long journey of Mediterranean-inspired meals with a sample menu plan that makes incorporating this wholesome diet into your routine easy and delicious.

Indulge in a variety of mouthwatering recipes crafted with the principles of the Mediterranean diet in mind. From energizing breakfasts to satisfying dinners, and delightful desserts and snacks, these recipes cater to a range of tastes, making every meal a celebration of flavor, nutrition, and the joy of savoring meals inspired by the Mediterranean lifestyle. Whether you are a seasoned cook or a beginner in the kitchen, this book is your guide to embracing a delicious and healthful approach to eating. May your culinary adventures be rich in flavor, nutrition, and the joy of savoring meals inspired by the Mediterranean lifestyle.

Contents

The Mediterranean diet is a diet inspired by the eating habits of countries around the Mediterranean Sea. The diet has been associated with improved health, including a lower risk of heart disease, cancer, Alzheimer's disease, and diabetes.

The Mediterranean diet is based on a diet of fruits, vegetables, whole grains, legumes, nuts, and olive oil. The diet also includes moderate consumption of fish, poultry, dairy, and red wine.

WHAT IS THE MEDITERRANEAN DIET?

The Mediterranean diet is a diet inspired by the eating habits of Greece, Southern Italy, and Spain. The diet traditionally includes vegetables, fruits, nuts, beans, cereals, olive oil, and fish.

The health benefits of the Mediterranean diet have been well-documented. Studies have shown that the Mediterranean diet can help reduce the risk of heart disease, stroke, and other chronic diseases. The diet has also been linked to a lower risk of Alzheimer's disease and cancer.

The Mediterranean diet is a healthy way to eat. It is based on foods that are naturally low in fat and cholesterol and high in nutrients. The diet is also low in processed foods and refined sugars.

The best way to follow the Mediterranean diet is to eat a variety of foods from all the food groups. Include plenty of fruits, vegetables, whole grains, beans, nuts, and seeds in your diet. Choose fish, poultry, and eggs as your main sources of protein. Use olive oil as your main source of fat. And limit your intake of red meat and processed meat.

The Mediterranean diet is a delicious way to eat healthily. The key to following the diet is to focus on eating fresh, whole foods. When you do that, you'll be on your way to enjoying all the health benefits the Mediterranean diet has to offer.

TOP HEALTH BENEFITS

For years, the Mediterranean Diet has been highly valued for its countless health benefits, the most prominent of which are discussed in detail below.

Protects Against Heart Disease

Heart disease accounts for more than 30%of deaths all over the world. One effective way to lower your risk of this disease is by taking on a healthy diet, such as the Mediterranean Diet.

Clinical studies have shown that this diet protects against heart problems by helping to stabilize cholesterol levels and preventing obesity.

Lowers Risk of Cancer

A disease characterized by uncontrollable growth and spread of malignant cells cancer is another leading cause of death worldwide.

There are many forms of cancer, some of which can be prevented with a diet that's rich in antioxidants.

As you might have heard, antioxidants can effectively fight the detrimental effects of free radicals in the body. Free radicals are some of the most common causes of inflammation and cancer.

In a 2004 study conducted by an Italian researcher, it was reported that the increased consumption of fruits and vegetables lowered the risk of digestive tract cancers. The Mediterranean Diet also appears to have a protective effect against cancers of the breast and the urinary tract.

Prevents Alzheimer's Disease

Alzheimer's Disease is a degenerative brain disease that can also be prevented with the help of the Mediterranean Diet.

Oily fish are rich in omega-3 fatty acids, which have been proven efficient in delaying the onset and progression of this debilitating disease.

Research published in the Annals of Neurology has shown that out of the 2,258 participants, those who adhered to the Mediterranean Diet were at much lower risk of Alzheimer's Disease compared to those who did not.

Scientists explain that the Mediterranean Diet works by keeping cholesterol and sugar levels in check, as well as strengthening the blood vessels. All these help in reducing the risk of both dementia and Alzheimer's Disease.

Prevents Parkinson's Disease

Another chronic ailment that can be prevented with this diet plan is Parkinson's Disease. This is possible through the high content of antioxidants that minimizes oxidative stress, which in turn leads to a reduction in the risk for this condition.

A 2014 clinical investigation confirmed that nutrition indeed plays an important role in the prevention of Parkinson's Disease.

Strengthens Muscles

If you want to stay strong and healthy even in your elderly years, the Mediterranean Diet is the way to go. This diet has been said to reduce muscle weakness and frailty by up to 70%.

Increases Life Span

By lowering the risk of life-threatening ailments such as heart disease, cancer and Alzheimer's Disease, there's a greater chance that you'll live a longer life. Following a Mediterranean Diet is said to reduce premature death by up to 20%.

GETTING TO KNOW ITS PRIMARY COMPONENTS

If you're convinced that the Mediterranean Diet is right for you, the first thing that you have to do is get to know about its extensive food list. This list enumerates the specific foods that you can consume regularly or moderately, and those that you should avoid completely.

Foods to Eat

Fruits and Vegetables

We've always been told to eat our veggies when we were kids, and now that you're about to start a Mediterranean Diet, you're going to be told the same thing.

Fruits and vegetables are packed with vitamins, minerals, fiber and antioxidants, all of which contribute to the reduction of cancer and heart disease risks, and promotion of overall health.

Some of the most nutritious and delicious fruits and veggies that you should include in your diet are apples, oranges, bananas, blueberries, strawberries, grapes, peaches, melons, figs, dates, pears, tomatoes, kale, spinach, onions, carrots, cauliflower, cucumbers and Brussels sprouts.

Whole Grains

Whole grains are good for you as they supply the body not only with dietary fiber but also with protein, vitamins and minerals.

These foods have been found to regulate digestion and decrease bowel issues. Moreover, these foods are also known to lower cholesterol.

Brown rice, oats, barley, corn, millet, and whole wheat are some good examples of whole grains that should be included in your daily menu.

Fish and Other Seafood

Mediterranean dieters avoid red meat for plenty of good reasons. Instead, they get their protein from fish and other types of seafood.

Fish, especially the oily varieties, contain vitamin A, vitamin D and omega-3 fatty acids that are linked to lower incidence of cancer, heart disease and Alzheimer's disease. These fatty acids also promote brain development and help in the management of depression and anxiety.

Cod, hake, halibut, salmon, tuna and plaice are some fish varieties that are popular in the Mediterranean Diet. You can also consume seafood like lobster, crabs, prawns and mussels, which are not only rich in protein but also in trace minerals.

Certain types of fish such as shark and swordfish should be avoided, as these have been found to contain mercury and other toxic heavy metals.

Legumes

The Mediterranean Diet encourages intake of legumes, which are also a type of vegetable but are grown in pods. These are packed with fiber, carbohydrates, protein and vitamins. Like other veggies, these are also said to prevent heart problems.

Use legumes like beans, chickpeas, peanuts, peas and lentils in your soup, stew or salad.

Fats and Oils

Saturated fats from animals including lard and butter are not recommended in the Mediterranean Diet. Instead, people use unsaturated oils, particularly olive oil.

Healthy fats can also be found in avocados and olives as well as from oils derived from nuts and seeds.

While it's true that the fat content of both Mediterranean and Western diets is almost the same, the former is linked to a lower rate of chronic diseases, mainly because of its focus on healthy fats.

Nuts and Seeds

Nuts and seeds are another excellent source of healthy unsaturated fats, vitamins, minerals, fiber and protein.

Make it a habit to snack on almonds, walnuts, cashews, chestnuts, Brazil nuts, Macadamia nuts, hazelnuts, pumpkin seeds, poppy seeds, sunflower seeds and sesame seeds.

White Meat

Another good alternative source of protein is lean poultry like chicken and turkey. Just use the white meat part and remove skin and fat.

Foods to Eat Moderately

Wine

Wine is a staple in the Mediterranean Diet. It is often used in pair with a dinner meal, or sometimes as an ingredient in cooking.

Red wine contains a potent antioxidant called resveratrol, which has been dubbed the "modern-day fountain of youth". It has many other antioxidants that also protect against cancer and heart ailments.

It's important to remember, however, that wine contains alcohol, which is why people are advised not to consume more than two glasses a day.

Poultry and Eggs

While you can eat plenty of white meat poultry, it's recommended that you consume other types of poultry as well as eggs in moderation.

Dairy Products

Dairy products such as milk, cheese, yogurt, butter and cream should not be consumed in large amounts.

Yes, these also contain essential nutrients such as calcium, protein, vitamin A and B vitamins. But we have to remember that these are also rich in saturated fat.

It helps if you opt for low-fat milk (skimmed milk) and low-fat cheeses (feta, mozzarella and cottage cheese).

Foods to Eat Only Rarely

Red meat

Meat lovers will be pleased to know that they don't have to say goodbye to red meat forever. It's all right to eat red meat such as pork, beef or lamb, but only from time to time.

Red meat is packed with protein and iron but is very high in saturated fat. Try to stay away from processed meat such as sausages and hotdogs which are even higher in fat and lower in nutrients.

Potatoes

Like other vegetables, potatoes are also rich in nutrients like B vitamins, vitamin C, potassium and dietary fiber. However, these are high in starch, which is known to be a precursor for type 2 diabetes. If you're going to include potatoes in your recipe, it would be healthier to boil or bake them.

Foods to Avoid

Sweets and Desserts

Here's the bad news for all sweet lovers out there: when you're on a Mediterranean Diet, you're going to be asked to avoid sugary treats and pastries as much as possible.

These include but are not limited to commercially produced cakes, cookies, brownies, and cupcakes. As you know, sugar shoots up the risk of type 2 diabetes.

But here's the upside: there are healthy alternatives to your favorite desserts, and we have rounded up some healthy dessert recipes in the next chapter.

Other Foods to Avoid

- Foods and drinks with added sugar - Soda, ice cream, hard and soft candies
- Refined grains - White bread, white rice, and pasta made with refined grains
- Foods with trans-fat - Margarine, cookies and other processed food products
- Refined oils - Canola oil, soybean oil, cottonseed oil
- Processed meat - Sausages, hot dogs, cold cuts
- Processed and instant food products

A Quick Guide on Portions

If you're wondering how much is plenty and how often is moderately, you'll find this daily portion guide helpful.

- Fruits: One piece of apple, orange or banana, 1 ounce of grapes, 7 ounces of melon
- Vegetables: One cup of raw vegetables or half a cup of cooked vegetables
- Legumes: One cup of cooked dry beans
- Potatoes: No more than 4 ounces
- Nuts and seeds: 1 ounce
- Lean Meat or Seafood: 2 ounces
- Whole Grains: One slice of bread or half a cup of rice or pasta
- Dairy: One cup of milk (preferably low-fat) or yogurt, 1 ounce of cheese
- Eggs: One egg
- Wine: One to two 125 ml. glasses

To conclude this section, here's the gist of the food list that you should consume before planning your menu.

What to Eat: Fruits, vegetables, legumes, nuts, seeds, whole grains, healthy oils, fish and seafood, lean poultry, herbs and spices

What to Eat Moderately: Wine, poultry, eggs, milk, cheese, yogurt

What to Eat Only Rarely: Red meat, potatoes

What Not to Eat: Sugary treats, pastries, soda, foods with added sugars, processed meat, instant food products, refined grains, and refined oils

MYTHS AND FACTS

Like other popular diet plans, there are also many myths surrounding the Mediterranean Diet. It's high time to bust these myths and get to know the real deal about this program.

Myth # 1: The Mediterranean Diet is Expensive

Fact: You don't have to break the bank with recipes that make use of vegetables like lentils and beans, whole grains like whole-wheat pasta and brown rice. In fact, it's much cheaper to go on this diet than to rely on the usual processed food products that other people buy.

Myth # 2: All Vegetable Oils are Healthy

Fact: It's not wise to grab any vegetable oil that you see in the supermarket. You have to be aware that vegetable oils come in two types.

The first one is the traditional cold-pressed oil such as peanut oil and olive oil. Packed with monounsaturated fat without the use of heat or chemicals for extraction, these are most commonly used in the Mediterranean Diet.

The second type is the modern processed oil. Examples of these are safflower oil, canola oil, corn oil and sunflower oil. Most of these oil products have been exposed to high heat and toxic chemicals, so it's best to steer clear of them.

Myth # 3: The More Wine You Drink, the Better

Fact: While it's true that red wine contains antioxidants that are good for you, it also contains alcohol, which as you know is not as healthy.

As mentioned earlier, it's wise to drink only a glass or two of red wine a day. This is how you can make the most out of its heart health benefits.

Myth # 4: Adopting a Mediterranean Diet Instantly Lowers Risk of Diseases

Fact: Although it has been proven in scientific research that the Mediterranean Diet can lower the risk of heart ailments and cancer, you can't achieve this without regular exercise and avoidance of unhealthy habits such as smoking.

Even if you are on this diet, but you smoke a lot or you live a sedentary lifestyle, you'll still be at risk of these diseases.

Myth # 5- Mediterranean Recipes are Complicated and Require Too Many Ingredients

Fact: As you'll see in the next chapter, Mediterranean recipes are not at all complicated. Most require the use of a few simple ingredients, and would only take a couple of minutes of your time. Even beginners or busy workers won't have any difficulty preparing these dishes.

MEDITERRANEAN DIET FOR WEIGHT LOss

Some people are so desperate to lose weight that they couldn't care less if the diet they're using may impair their health in the long run. The only thing that matters to them is that they drop the unwanted pounds fast.

But you know better. You know that weight loss takes time and that it's better to lose weight gradually, as long as it's permanent, instead of dropping pounds quickly only to gain them back after a few days or weeks.

The Mediterranean Diet guarantees safe and effective weight loss for the long term. How does it work? Here are some of the ways it helps you slim down:

- Cuts down on caloric intake
- Minimizes intake of unhealthy fats
- Lowers consumption of carbohydrates
- Encourages physical activity
- Promotes nutritionally-dense foods that provide energy for exercise
- Promotes healthy lifestyle habits

Several studies have shown that the Mediterranean Diet is indeed effective as a weight loss program.

In a 2011 study, researchers evaluated a total of 16 clinical trials involving over 3,400 individuals. It was found that the 1,848 participants assigned to the Mediterranean Diet lost more weight and experienced a more significant increase in physical activity than the other participants.

Another study published in the British Journal of Nutrition reported that following the Mediterranean Diet resulted in both weight loss and decreased cholesterol levels.

These and many others studies serve as proof that the Mediterranean Diet is indeed an effective tool for dropping pounds and maintaining ideal weight.

HOw TO GET STARTED

Changing your diet habits in an instant is never easy. That's why starting a new diet program can be nerve-wracking for many people.

With the Mediterranean Diet, you're not required to have a major overhaul of your routine overnight. You can start slowly. Here are some ways you can gradually transition to this diet plan.

Include More Fruits and Vegetables in Your Diet

It's not as difficult as it sounds. Just make a conscious effort to go for foods that will steer you towards fruits and vegetables.

Making pizza? Top it with sliced tomatoes, olives and basil instead of the usual pepperoni and ham that you put in there. Cooking dinner? Make it a habit to pair it with a bowl of fresh green salad. Thinking about a cold smoothie? Put kale, spinach and other leafy greens in your blender to make a healthy green smoothie.

Go for Healthy Protein Sources

Always keep in mind that red meat is not the only possible source of protein. Legumes, nuts, seeds, yogurt, lean poultry and seafood are also rich in this nutrient.

If you're going to eat meat, go for organic and grass-fed meat so you can stay away from the hormones and antibiotics that commercial meat is loaded with.

As much as possible, limit your intake. For example, it's better to top your salad or pasta with small strips of beef instead of devouring a thick slice of prime rib steak.

Don't Skip Your Breakfast

A common mistake committed by dieters: skipping breakfast. If you think that you're doing yourself a favor skipping the most important meal of the day, you're not.

When the body is in slumber, the metabolism slows down so that you won't get hungry in the middle of the night. But you have to eat something in the morning to "break the fast".

Otherwise, the body will think it's not going to get any food soon, and will go into starvation mode. This slows down the metabolism once again, and hinders burning of fat and calories—something that no dieter wants.

Start your day right with a breakfast of whole grains, fruits and vegetables. It's also good to eat eggs or drink milk, but minimize intake as much as you can.

Have Vegetarian Nights at Home

You don't have to completely ban meat in your home. But to make it easier for you to skip on meat, try having vegetarian nights. Pick one or two days in a week in which you will cook and serve vegetarian dishes only.

So that everyone looks forward to these nights (instead of dreading them), make sure you prepare luscious and appetizing meals that your family will enjoy.

Go for Low-Fat Dairy Products

Dairy products are allowed in the Mediterranean Diet program. However, you'll be asked to consume these moderately. And whenever possible, go for those that are lower in fat and are organic.

Treat Yourself with Healthy Sweets

Cakes, cookies and pastries are not the only ones that can satisfy your cravings for sweets. You can also get the same level of satisfaction from fresh fruits and berries. And in place of ice cream, eat chilled yogurt topped with fruits instead.

TIPs FOR SHOPPING AND EATING IN REsTAURANTs

Doing your grocery shopping and eating in restaurants can be tricky when you're on a diet. But you can make things easier for yourself with the help of these practical suggestions:

When Eating Out

- Ask the waiter not to bring appetizers like bread and biscuits.
- Don't order anything that's fried.
- Choose dishes made with seafood, lean meat or poultry. Or better yet, look for something vegetarian.
- Go for mixed salads, steamed fish, grilled vegetables and soups.
- If you can't help but order beef, go for sirloin, flake, filet mignon or tenderloin. These are less fatty than other cuts.
- Inquire about the sauce. Ask the waiter what the base of the sauce is. If there's butter or cream in the sauce, skip it. Opt for something that's made with olive oil or tomato instead.
- Request for ingredient substitution. There are many restaurants that are willing to make minor changes in their dishes. For example, if you'd like to order pasta, instead of having bacon as the topping, you can ask for lean chicken or tuna flakes instead.
- Order healthier side dishes like baked potato, steamed vegetables or fresh green salad in lieu of potato chips, French fries or mashed potatoes.
- Don't finish your plate. Eat only half of what you ordered and take home the rest.

- Practice mindful eating. Chew your food slowly and give yourself time to enjoy each bite. This will make you feel full sooner.
- Order fresh fruits or berries for dessert.
- Drink non-caloric beverages such as water, tea, fresh fruit or vegetable juice, or sugar-free soda.
- If you're going to drink alcohol, limit it to one or two drinks.

When Grocery Shopping

- Create your menu at home. Make a grocery shopping list based on the ingredients required in these recipes. Having a grocery list helps you avoid temptations.
- Buy only organic food products. Try your best to avoid anything that's heavily processed.
- Shop at the store's perimeter, where you can find the whole foods.
- Don't linger in the sweets or chips section long enough to get yourself tempted in loading your cart with unhealthy treats.

SAMPLE WEEKLY MENU PLAN

Here's a sample weekly menu plan that you can try:

Monday

- Breakfast – Egg and Mushroom Pesto
- Lunch – Seared Tuna Steaks
- Snacks/Dessert – Yogurt Popsicle
- Dinner – Tuscan Tuna Salad

Tuesday

- Breakfast – Yogurt with Berries and Walnuts
- Lunch – Lemon Chicken
- Snacks/Dessert – Plum Cake
- Dinner – Flank Steak Gyros

Wednesday

- Breakfast – Oatmeal with Fruits
- Lunch – Zucchini Gnocchi
- Snacks/Dessert – Dolma Wrap
- Dinner – Tomato and Corn Soup

Thursday

- Breakfast – Breakfast Sandwiches
- Lunch – Broiled Salmon with Mustard
- Snacks/Dessert – Vegetable Pizza
- Dinner – Artichoke and Olive Salad

Friday

- Breakfast - Asparagus Prosciutto with Egg
- Lunch – Greek Sardine Salad

- Snacks/Dessert – Watermelon Sorbet
- Dinner – Grilled Calamari with Veggie Salad

Saturday

- Breakfast – Breakfast Couscous
- Lunch – Garlic Shrimp Pasta
- Snacks/Dessert – White Bean Spread on Crackers
- Dinner – Sautéed Squash and Gorgonzola Polenta

Sunday

- Breakfast – Breakfast Quinoa
- Lunch – Savory Tofu with Rice Soup
- Snacks/Dessert – Pears in Wine
- Dinner – Salmon with Apple Walnut Salad

RECIPES

15 RECIPES FOR BREAKFAST
BREAKFAST QUINOA
Yields: 4 servings

Ingredients

- ¼ cup almonds, chopped
- 1 cup quinoa
- 1 tsp. ground cinnamon
- 1 tsp. salt
- 2 cups low-fat milk
- 5 dried apricots, chopped
- 2 dried pitted dates, chopped

- 2 tbsp. honey
- 1 tsp. vanilla extract

Instructions

1. Put a skillet over medium high heat.
2. Toast the almonds for three to five minutes, set aside.
3. In a saucepan over medium heat, warm the quinoa and ground cinnamon.
4. Sprinkle salt and pour in the milk.
5. Bring to a boil then simmer for 15 minutes.
6. Add dates, apricots, honey and vanilla extract.
7. Add half of the toasted almonds.
8. Mix well.
9. Top with the other half of the almonds before serving.

Nutritional Information per Serving:

Calories 327
Fat 7g
Carbs 51.8g
Fiber 5.2g
Sugar 21.9g
Protein 12.1g

ASPARAGUS PROSCIUTTO WITH EGG

Yields: 4 servings

Ingredients

- 8 stalks fresh asparagus, trimmed
- 2 tbsp. olive oil, divided

- 2 oz. prosciutto, minced
- Pinch of salt and pepper
- 1 tsp. distilled white vinegar
- 4 eggs

Instructions

1. Preheat your oven to 425°F.
2. Put asparagus stalks on a baking pan.
3. Drizzle with one tbsp. olive oil.
4. In a pan over medium heat, warm the remaining olive oil.
5. Cook prosciutto until golden.
6. Add to the baking pan.
7. Season with pepper. Toss.
8. Roast in the oven for 10 minutes.
9. Toss and put it back in the oven to roast for five minutes more.
10. In a saucepan, poach eggs.
11. Serve roasted asparagus and prosciutto with eggs.

Nutritional Information per Serving:

Calories 144
Fat 12.2g
Carbs 0.6g
Fiber 0g
Sugar 0g
PROTEIN 8.5G

EGG AND MUSHROOM PESTO
Yields: 1 serving

Ingredients

- 1 tsp. olive oil
- 1 Portobello mushroom cap, sliced
- 1 onion, chopped
- 4 egg whites
- 1 tsp. water
- Pinch of salt and pepper
- ¼ cup reduced-fat mozzarella cheese, shredded
- 1 tsp. pesto sauce
- ¼ cup oil

Instructions

1. In a skillet over medium low heat, pour olive oil.
2. Cook mushroom and onion for three to five minutes.
3. Whisk egg and water in a bowl. Add to the skillet.
4. Sprinkle salt and pepper to taste.
5. Stir occasionally until eggs have become firm.
6. Top with mozzarella and pesto cheese.
7. Fold egg, cook for three minutes more, and then serve.

Nutritional Information per Serving:

Calories 330
Fat 30.9g
Carbs 6.1g
Fiber 1.3g
Sugar 3.1g
Protein 8.3g

CHAKCHOUKA
Yields: 4 servings

Ingredients

- 3 tbsp. olive oil
- 2 cloves garlic, minced
- 2 red bell peppers, sliced
- 1 onion, chopped
- 2 tomatoes, chopped
- 1 tsp. salt
- 1 tsp. paprika
- 1 tsp. ground cumin
- 1 chili pepper, chopped
- 4 eggs

Instructions

1. Pour olive oil in a pan over medium low heat.
2. Sauté garlic, bell peppers and onions for three to five minutes.
3. In a bowl, mix tomatoes, salt, paprika, cumin and chili pepper.
4. Add mixture to the pan.
5. Stir and cook for 10 minutes.
6. Crack four eggs into the pan.
7. Cover the skillet and cook eggs for five minutes.
8. Serve while warm.

Nutritional Information per Serving:
Calories 200
Fat 15.4g
Carbs 10.9g

Fiber 2.5g
Sugar 6.3g
Protein 7.3g

YOGURT WITH BERRIES AND WALNUTS

Yields: 1 serving

Ingredients

- 1 cup low-fat yogurt
- ½ cup blueberries, sliced
- ½ cup strawberries, sliced
- ¼ cup walnuts, chopped
- 1 tbsp. honey

Instructions

1. Put berry slices on top of the yogurt.
2. Sprinkle chopped walnuts.
3. Pour honey.
4. Chill in the refrigerator for a few minutes before serving.

Nutritional Information per Serving:

Calories 360
Fat 19g
Carbs 26g
Fiber 3g
Sugar 16g
Protein 28g

BREAKFAST COUSCOUS

Yields: 4 servings

Ingredients

- 1 tsp. ground cinnamon
- 3 cups skimmed milk
- 1 cup whole-wheat couscous (uncooked)
- ¼ cup dried currants
- ½ cup dried apricots, chopped
- ¼ tsp. salt
- 6 tsp. brown sugar, divided
- 4 tsp. low-fat butter, melted and divided

Instructions

1. Put a pan over medium high heat.
2. Mix cinnamon and milk in a bowl, and then transfer to the pan.
3. Heat for three minutes.
4. Turn off the heat.
5. Add couscous, currants and apricots.
6. Season with salt and four tsp. sugar.
7. Cover with the lid and let it sit for 15 minutes.
8. Pour mixture in four bowls.
9. Top with butter and remaining sugar.

Nutritional Information per Serving:

Calories 306

Fat 6g

Carbs 55g

Fiber 5g

Sugar 0g

Protein 11g

BREAKFAST SANDWICHES

Yields: 4 servings

Ingredients

- 4 slices whole-wheat bread
- 4 tsp. olive oil
- ½ tsp. dried rosemary leaves, crushed
- 4 eggs
- 2 cups fresh spinach leaves
- 1 tomato, sliced
- 4 tbsp. feta cheese
- Pinch of salt and pepper

Instructions

1. Preheat your oven to 375°F.
2. Brush each bread slice with a little olive oil.
3. Place on the baking pan and toast inside the oven for five minutes.
4. In a skillet over medium high heat, put remaining olive oil and add rosemary.
5. Crack one egg at a time into the skillet.
6. Cook for about a minute.
7. Flip the eggs to cook the other side.
8. Remove from the stove.
9. Put bread on a cutting board.
10. Put spinach, tomato, eggs and feta cheese on each bread.
11. Season with salt and pepper.
12. Top with the other bread slice.
13. Slice the sandwich into two.

Nutritional Information per Serving:

Calories 242
Fat 12g
Carbs 25g
Fiber 6g
Sugar 3g
Protein 13g

SALTED BREAKFAST POTATOES
Yields: 4 servings

Ingredients
For the salt:

- ¼ cup salt
- ½ cup oregano
- ¼ cup cinnamon
- 1 cup fresh rosemary leaves
- ¼ cup paprika

For the potatoes:

- 2 potatoes, peeled and diced
- 1 tbsp. low-fat butter
- 1 tbsp. oil

Instructions

1. Put salt, oregano, cinnamon, rosemary and paprika in a spice grinder.
2. Grind until consistency is smooth.
3. In a pan, heat oil and butter.

4. Cook potatoes.
5. Drain the potatoes and coat with herbs and salt.

Nutritional Information per Serving:

Calories 190
Fat 13g
Carbs 19g
Fiber 4g
Sugar 1g
Protein 2g

CHEESY SPINACH MUFFIN

Yields: 6 servings

Ingredients

- Cooking oil spray
- 4 tbsp. Parmesan cheese, grated
- 2 tbsp. skimmed milk
- 1 tomato, seeded and chopped
- 1 ounce spinach, finely chopped
- 1 ounce leeks, chopped
- Salt and pepper to taste
- 1 ounce low-fat cheddar cheese, grated

Instructions

1. Preheat your oven to 375°F.
2. Coat muffin pan with cooking oil spray.
3. In a bowl, combine milk and parmesan cheese.
4. Add all the vegetables.

5. Mix well.
6. Divide mixture into the muffin pan.
7. Top with grated cheddar cheese.
8. Bake for 15 to 20 minutes.

Nutritional Information per Serving:

Calories 350
Fat 25g
Carbs 12g
Fiber 3g
Sugar 0g
Protein 20g

TOASTED BREAD WITH TUNA

Yields: 2 servings

Ingredients

- 3 tbsp. low-fat mayonnaise
- ½ onion, chopped
- ¼ cup tuna flakes
- Salt and pepper to taste
- 2 slices of whole-wheat bread

Instructions

1. In a bowl, combine mayo, onion and tuna flakes.
2. Season with salt and pepper.
3. Spread on whole-wheat bread.
4. Toast in the oven for a few minutes until golden and crispy.

Nutritional Information per Serving:

Calories 155
Fat 8.5g
Carbs 15.7g
Fiber 2.5g
Sugar 2.7g
Protein 3.9g

OATMEAL WITH FRUITS

Yields: 1 serving

Ingredients

- 1 cup rolled oats
- ¼ cup strawberries, sliced
- 1 banana, sliced
- 1 tbsp. honey
- ¼ cup low-fat milk

Instructions

1. Cook rolled oats in boiling water.
2. Remove from heat.
3. Top with fruit slices
4. Drizzle with milk and honey before serving.

Nutritional Information per Serving:

Calories 206
Fat 3g
Carbs 39.2g

Fiber 4.5g
Sugar 0g
Protein 6.6g

CRANBERRY BREAD

Yields: 4 servings

Ingredients

- 2 avocados, peeled and seeded
- 3 oz. feta, crumbled
- 2 tbsp. mint, chopped
- 1 tsp. lemon juice
- Salt and pepper to taste

Instructions

1. Put avocado in a bowl.
2. Use a fork to mash.
3. Add mint and lemon juice.
4. Season with salt and pepper.
5. Toast bread in the oven.
6. Spread avocado mixture on the bread slice.
7. Top with feta cheese before serving.

Nutritional Information per Serving:

Calories 259
Fat 23.9g
Carbs 9.8g
Fiber 6.9g
Sugar 1.3g

Protein 4.8g

WALNUT AND DATE OATS

Yields: 1 serving

Ingredients

- ½ cup rolled oats, cooked
- 1 tbsp. chia seeds
- 2 tbsp. walnuts, chopped
- ¾ cup almond milk
- 1 tbsp. vanilla protein powder
- 2 to 3 dates, chopped
- ½ tsp. cinnamon

Instructions

1. Put all the ingredients in a glass jar with lid.
2. Shake to blend well.
3. Secure the jar with the lid and refrigerate overnight.
4. The next day, reheat in the microwave before eating.

Nutritional Information per Serving:

Calories 345
Fat 17g
Carbs 38g
Fiber 0g
Sugar 8g
Protein 16g

CARAMELIZED FIGS WITH PISTACHIOS

Yields: 4 servings

Ingredients

- 1 tbsp. honey
- 8 oz. fresh figs, cut into half
- 2 cups low-fat Greek yogurt
- ⅛ tsp. ground cinnamon
- ¼ cup pistachios, chopped

Instructions

1. Put skillet over medium heat.
2. Heat honey and add figs for five minutes.
3. Pour over yogurt.
4. Top with pistachios and cinnamon before serving.

Nutritional Information per Serving:

Calories 177
Fat 2.3g
Carbs 41.6g
Fiber 6g
Sugar 31.7g
Protein 2.6g

PANCAKE WITH STRAWBERRY YOGURT

Yields: 5 servings

Ingredients

- 1 cup whole-wheat pancake mix
- 1 egg
- ¾ cup fat-free milk

- 1 cup low-fat yogurt
- 1 cup fresh strawberries, chopped

Instructions

1. Beat egg and add to pancake mix.
2. Stir in milk.
3. Cook pancake in a skillet.
4. Flip to cook the other side.
5. Top yogurt with strawberries and serve with pancake.

Nutritional Information per Serving:

Calories 135
Fat 1.5g
Carbs 4.1g
Fiber 6g
Sugar 3.3g
Protein 2.5g

15 RECIPES FOR LUNCH

GARLIC SHRIMP PASTA

Yields: 3 servings

Ingredients

- 6 oz. whole-wheat spaghetti
- 2 tbsp. olive oil, divided
- 1 bunch asparagus, trimmed and sliced
- 12 oz. shrimp, peeled and deveined
- 1 cup frozen peas

- 3 cloves garlic, chopped
- 1 red bell pepper, sliced
- Salt and pepper to taste
- 2 cups non-fat yogurt
- ¼ cup parsley
- 3 tbsp. lemon juice

Instructions

1. Cook pasta according to package directions.
2. Strain and set aside.
3. In a pan, cook shrimp, bell pepper, asparagus and peas in half of the olive oil.
4. Cook for two to four minutes or until shrimp is tender. Set aside.
5. In a blender, grind garlic and salt.
6. Add yogurt, parsley, lemon juice, remaining olive oil and pepper into the blender.
7. Pulse some more.
8. Put pasta in a mixing bowl.
9. Add sauce and toss to coat.
10. Top with shrimp and vegetables before serving.

Nutritional Information per Serving:

Calories 361
Fat 6g
Carbs 53g
Fiber 10g
Sugar 14g
Protein 28g

ZUCCHINI GNOCCHI
Yields: 4 servings

Ingredients

- 1 lb. fresh gnocchi
- 2 tbsp. butter
- 1 lb. zucchini, sliced lengthwise
- 2 shallots, chopped
- 1 pint cherry tomatoes, cut into half
- ¼ tsp. nutmeg, grated
- Pinch of salt and pepper
- ½ cup fresh parsley, chopped
- ½ cup Parmesan cheese, grated

Instructions

1. Cook gnocchi according to package directions.
2. Drain and set aside.
3. In a skillet over medium high heat, melt butter.
4. Wait for two minutes before adding zucchini and shallots.
5. Cook for two to three minutes.
6. Add cherry tomatoes, nutmeg, salt and pepper.
7. Cook for another two minutes.
8. Add parsley and Parmesan.
9. Add gnocchi and stir to coat.

Nutritional Information per Serving:
Calories 426
Fat 11g
Carbs 66g
Fiber 4g

Sugar 0g
Protein 17g

BROILED SALMON WITH MUSTARD
Yields: 4 servings

Ingredients

- 1¼ lb. salmon fillets
- ¼ tsp. salt
- ¼ tsp. pepper
- 2 tbsp. mustard
- ¼ cup low-fat sour cream
- 2 tsp. lemon juice
- Lemon wedges
- Fresh parsley, chopped

Instructions

1. Preheat your broiler.
2. Line your baking pan with foil.
3. Coat with cooking spray.
4. Lay salmon fillet pieces on the pan.
5. Season with salt and pepper.
6. In a bowl, mix mustard, sour cream and lemon juice.
7. Spread this on both sides of the salmon fillet.
8. Broil salmon for 10 minutes.
9. Garnish with lemon wedges and fresh parsley before serving.

Nutritional Information per Serving:
Calories 198

Fat 8g
Carbs 2g
Fiber 0g
Sugar 1g
Protein 29g

LEMON CHICKEN
Yields: 4 servings

Ingredients

- Salt and pepper to taste
- 4 fillets chicken breast (boneless and skinless)
- 3 tsp. olive oil
- 3 cloves garlic, minced
- 1 onion, chopped
- 2 tsp. flour
- 1 cup low-sodium chicken stock
- 1 tbsp. lemon juice
- 2 tbsp. fresh dill, chopped

Instructions

1. Rub salt and pepper on both sides of chicken.
2. In a pan over medium high heat, pour olive oil and brown chicken on both sides.
3. Transfer chicken to a serving platter.
4. Cover with foil.
5. Lower heat to medium.
6. Sauté onion and garlic for one minute.
7. In a bowl, mix dill, lemon juice, flour and stock.

8. Pour into the pan.
9. Cook for three minutes.
   10. Put chicken back into the pan.
   11. Reduce heat and simmer for four minutes.

Nutritional Information per Serving:

Calories 170
Fat 6g
Carbs 3g
Fiber 0g
Sugar 1g
Protein 24g

VEGETABLE HOAGIES

Yields: 4 servings

Ingredients

- ¼ cup onion, sliced into rings
- 1 tbsp. oil
- 2 tbsp. balsamic vinegar
- 1 tomato, diced
- 14 oz. canned artichoke hearts, rinsed and chopped
- 1 tsp. dried oregano
- 1 whole-grain baguette
- 2 slices provolone cheese
- 2 cups Romaine lettuce, shredded

Instructions

1. Fill a small bowl with cold water.

2. Add onion rings into the bowl, and set aside.
3. In another bowl, mix oil, balsamic vinegar, tomato and artichoke hearts.
4. Slice baguette into four.
5. Get the onions from the water and pat them dry.
6. On each bread, put cheese, artichoke mixture, onion ring and lettuce.
7. Cover with other bread slice.

Nutritional Information per Serving:
Calories 266
Fat 8g
Carbs 40g
Fiber 8g
Sugar 4g
Protein 14g

GREEK SARDINE SALAD

Yields: 4 servings

Ingredients

- 2 tbsp. oil
- 3 tbsp. lemon juice
- ½ tsp. pepper
- 1 tsp. dried oregano
- 1 clove garlic, minced
- 1 cucumber, sliced
- 3 tomatoes, quarter cut
- ⅓ cup feta cheese, crumbled
- 15 oz. canned chickpeas, rinsed and drained
- 2 tbsp. olives, sliced
- ¼ cup red onion, sliced
- 4 oz. canned sardines

Instructions

1. Combine oil, lemon juice, pepper, oregano and garlic in a bowl.
2. Add cucumber, tomatoes, cheese, chickpeas, olive and onion.
3. Toss gently.
4. Top with sardines before serving.

Nutritional Information per Serving:

Calories 347
Fat 18g
Carbs 29g
Fiber 6g
Sugar 6g

Protein 17g

CHICKEN SALAD
Yields: 2 servings

Ingredients

- 1 tbsp. olive oil
- 2½ tbsp. red wine vinegar
- 1½ tsp. fresh dill, chopped
- Salt and pepper to taste
- ½ tsp. garlic powder
- 1 cucumber, peeled and chopped
- 1 tomato, chopped
- 3 cups Romaine lettuce, chopped
- 1 cup cooked chicken, chopped
- ¼ cup black olives, sliced
- ¼ cup onion, chopped
- ¼ cup feta cheese, crumbled

Instructions

1. Mix oil, vinegar, dill, salt, pepper and garlic powder in a big salad bowl.
2. Add cucumber, tomato, lettuce, chicken, olives and onion.
3. Toss to coat.
4. Top with feta cheese before serving.

Nutritional Information per Serving:
Calories 343
Fat 18g
Carbs 11g
Fiber 3g
Sugar 5g

Protein 31g

GRILLED SHRIMP WITH BEAN AND TOMATO SALAD

Yields: 6 servings

Ingredients

- 3 tbsp. olive oil
- ⅓ cup lemon juice
- 1 tsp. lemon zest
- 2 tbsp. sage, minced
- 2 tbsp. fresh chives, minced
- 2 tbsp. fresh oregano, minced
- ½ tsp. salt
- 1 tsp. pepper
- 12 cherry tomatoes, quarter cut
- 15 oz. canned cannellini beans, rinsed and drained
- 24 pieces raw shrimp, peeled and deveined

Instructions

1. In a bowl, mix oil, lemon juice, lemon zest, sage, chives, oregano, salt and pepper.
2. Add tomatoes and beans to the bowl.
3. Toss to coat.
4. Preheat the grill.
5. Put shrimp on skewers and grill for four minutes.
6. Serve with salad.

Nutritional Information per Serving:

Calories 212
Fat 8g
Carbs 22g
Fiber 8g
Sugar 2g

Protein 17g

SAVORY TOFU AND RICE SOUP

Yields: 4 servings

Ingredients

- ⅓ cup white rice
- 4 cups low-sodium chicken stock
- 1 tbsp. olive oil
- ¼ tsp. turmeric
- 1½ cups silken tofu
- 2 tbsp. fresh dill, chopped
- ¼ tsp. freshly ground pepper
- ¼ cup lemon juice

Instructions

1. Put rice and stock in a large saucepan.
2. Bring to a boil.
3. Lower heat and simmer for 15 minutes.
4. Put rice in a blender.
5. Add oil, turmeric and tofu.
6. Blend until consistency is smooth.
7. Put mixture in a pot.
8. Add dill, pepper and lemon juice.
9. Simmer for 15 minutes before serving.

Nutritional Information per Serving:

Calories 163
Fat 6g
Carbs 19g
Fiber 0g
Sugar 2g
Protein 9g

SEARED TUNA STEAK
Yields: 4 servings

Ingredients

- ½ tsp. ground coriander
- Salt and pepper to taste
- 4 yellow fin tuna steaks
- 1 tsp. olive oil
- 1½ cups tomato, chopped
- ¼ cup green onion, chopped
- 3 tbsp. fresh parsley, chopped
- 1 tbsp. capers, drained
- 1 tbsp. lemon juice
- 1 tbsp. olive oil
- 12 chopped pitted Kalamata olives

Instructions

1. Rub coriander, salt and pepper on both sides of tuna steaks.
2. In a skillet over medium heat, pour one tsp. of olive oil.
3. Cook fish four minutes on each side.
4. Combine all the remaining ingredients in a bowl.
5. Pour mixture on top of the fish.

Nutritional Information per Serving:
Calories 268
Fat 8.4g
Carbs 5.8g
Fiber 1.4g
Sugar 0g
Protein 40.9g

LAMB, TURKEY AND CHICKPEA CHILI
Yields: 2 servings

Ingredients

- 1 tsp. olive oil
- 2 cloves garlic, minced
- ½ onion, chopped
- 1 red bell pepper, chopped
- 4 oz. ground lamb
- 4 oz. lean ground turkey
- Salt to taste
- 7 oz. canned chickpeas, rinsed and drained
- 2 tomatoes, chopped
- ⅛ tsp. ground cinnamon
- 1½ tsp. chili powder
- 1 tbsp. fresh mint, chopped

Instructions

1. In a saucepan over medium heat, pour olive oil and sauté garlic, onion and red bell pepper until soft.
2. Add turkey, lamb and salt. Cook for about four minutes.
3. Add tomatoes and cook for another four minutes.
4. Lastly, add chili powder, chickpeas, and cinnamon, and cook for one minute.
5. Garnish with fresh mint before serving.

Nutritional Information per Serving:
Calories 356
Fat 16g
Carbs 28g
Fiber 6g

Sugar 5g
Protein 26g

KALE AND BEAN SOUP
Yields: 8 servings

Ingredients

- 1 tbsp. olive oil
- 10 oz. sausage, sliced
- 1 cup onion, chopped
- 2 tbsp. garlic, minced
- 1 cup carrot, chopped
- 6 cups low-sodium chicken stock
- 14 oz. canned diced tomatoes
- 1 lb. small potatoes, sliced
- 1 tbsp. fresh marjoram, chopped
- 15 oz. canned kidney beans, rinsed and drained
- 1 lb. kale, stems removed and chopped
- ½ cup chopped fresh parsley
- Salt and pepper to taste

Instructions

1. Put olive oil in a pot over medium high heat.
2. Brown sausage for four to five minutes.
3. Put sausage on a serving platter.
4. Add carrot and onion to the pot.
5. Cover and cook for 10 minutes.
6. Add garlic and cook for one more minute.
7. Pour in the stock and tomatoes.
8. Bring to a boil.

9. Add potatoes and simmer for 10 minutes.
10. Add sausage, beans, kale and parsley.
11. Simmer for four to five minutes more.
12. Sprinkle with salt and pepper.

Nutritional Information per Serving:

Calories 279
Fat 8g
Carbs 34g
Fiber 8g
Sugar 5g
Protein 19g

CHORIZO PILAF

Yields: 4 servings

Ingredients

- 1 tbsp. olive oil
- 1 onion, sliced
- 9 oz. chorizo, sliced
- 1 tsp. smoked paprika
- 4 cloves garlic, crushed
- ¾ lb. canned chopped tomatoes
- 9 oz. basmati rice
- 2½ cups chicken stock
- ¼ tsp. lemon zest
- Lemon wedges
- 1 tbsp. parsley, chopped
- 2 fresh bay leaves

Instructions

1. Pour oil in a pan.
2. Sauté onion and cook until soft.
3. Move to one side of the pan.
4. Put chorizo into the pan and cook until brown.
5. Add paprika, garlic and tomatoes.
6. Mix all the ingredients.
7. Cook for five minutes.
8. Add rice, lemon zest, bay leaves and stock.
9. Bring to a boil.
10. Cover and simmer for 12 minutes.
11. Garnish with parsley and lemon wedges before serving.

Nutritional Information per Serving:

Calories 488
Fat 18g
Carbs 58g
Fiber 3g
Sugar 9g
Protein 19g

CAPONATA

Yields: 8 servings

Ingredients

- ⅓ cup olive oil
- 3 eggplants, cubed
- 2 shallots, chopped

- 4 tomatoes, chopped
- 2 oz. raisins
- 2 tsp. unsalted capers
- 3 tbsp. red wine vinegar
- 4 sticks celery, sliced
- ½ cup pine nuts, toasted
- ½ cup basil leaves, chopped
- 8 slices ciabatta
- 1 tbsp. olive oil
- 1 clove garlic, crushed

Instructions

1. Warm olive oil in a pot over medium heat.
2. Cook eggplants for 20 minutes.
3. Remove eggplants from the pan.
4. Add shallots and cook for five minutes.
5. Add tomatoes and cook for 15 minutes.
6. Put back the eggplants and add raisins, capers, wine vinegar and celery.
7. Cover with the lid and simmer on low heat for 40 minutes.
8. While waiting, brush olive oil on the bread and rub garlic clove.
9. Grill the bread.
   10. Garnish stew with nuts and basil.
   11. Serve stew with the bread.

Nutritional Information per Serving:
Calories 235
Fat 15g
Carbs 20g
Fiber 5g

Sugar 8g
Protein 4g

HERBED LAMB AND ROASTED VEGGIES
Yields: 4 servings

Ingredients

- 1 onion, quarter cut
- 2 red bell peppers, chopped
- 2 zucchinis, sliced
- 1 sweet potato, peeled and chopped
- 1 tbsp. olive oil
- Pepper to taste
- 2 tbsp. mint leaves, chopped
- 1 tbsp. thyme leaf, chopped
- 8 lean lamb cutlets (fat removed)

Instructions

1. Preheat your oven to 425°F.
2. In a baking pan, put onion, pepper, zucchini and sweet potato.
3. Put inside the oven and roast for five minutes.
4. Drizzle with oil and sprinkle with black pepper.
5. Combine mint, thyme and pepper.
6. Use this to season the lamb cutlets.
7. Get the pan out of the oven and push vegetables to one side.
8. Put lamb cutlets in the middle and put back in the oven.
9. Roast until lamb is tender.

Nutritional Information per Serving:

Calories 429
Fat 29g
Carbs 23g
Fiber 6g
Sugar 12g
Protein 19g

15 RECIPES FOR DINNER
TUSCAN TUNA SALAD

Yields: 4 servings

Ingredients

- 6 oz. canned light tuna flakes, drained
- 4 scallions, sliced
- 10 cherry tomatoes, quarter cut
- 2 tbsp. lemon juice
- 2 tbsp. olive oil
- ¼ tsp. salt
- 15 oz. canned white beans
- Pepper to taste

Instructions

1. Put tuna flakes, scallions, tomatoes, lemon juice, olive oil, salt and pepper in a bowl.
2. Toss to coat.
3. Chill in the refrigerator for a few minutes before serving.

Nutritional Information per Serving:

Calories 199
Fat 9g
Carbs 20g
Fiber 6g
Sugar 2g
Protein 16g

RAVIOLI AND VEGETABLE SOUP

Yields: 4 servings

Ingredients

- 1 tbsp. olive oil
- 1 cup onion, diced
- 2 cloves garlic, minced
- 1 cup bell pepper, diced
- ¼ tsp. red pepper, crushed
- 15 oz. canned vegetable stock
- 28 oz. canned crushed tomatoes
- 1½ cups hot water
- 1 tsp. dried basil
- 9 oz. frozen cheese whole-wheat ravioli
- 2 cups zucchini, diced
- Pepper to taste

Instructions

1. Pour olive oil in a saucepan over medium heat.
2. Cook onion, garlic, red pepper and bell pepper for one to two minutes.
3. Add vegetable stock, tomatoes, water and basil.

4. Bring to a boil.
5. Add ravioli and cook according to package directions.
6. Add zucchini and cook for three minutes.
7. Sprinkle with pepper before serving.

Nutritional Information per Serving:

Calories 261
Fat 8g
Carbs 33g
Fiber 7g
Sugar 12g
Protein 11g

SPAGHETTI FRITTATA

Yields: 6 servings

Ingredients

- 4 cups cooked spaghetti
- 4 tsp. olive oil
- 3 onions, chopped
- 4 eggs
- ⅓ cup Parmesan cheese, grated
- ½ cup non-fat milk
- 2 tbsp. basil, chopped
- 2 tbsp. parsley, chopped
- 1 tsp. salt
- ½ tsp. pepper
- 1 tomato, diced

Instructions

1. Heat oil in a skillet over medium heat.
2. Cook onion for 10 minutes.
3. Transfer onions in a bowl.
4. Beat in eggs and milk into the bowl.
5. Add Parmesan, basil, parsley, salt and pepper.
6. Put back the pan on the stove.
7. Reduce heat to low.
8. Add spaghetti.
9. Pour egg mixture on top.
    10. Cover the pan with a lid.
    11. Wait for the eggs to set.
    12. Invert on a platter before serving.

Nutritional Information per Serving:

Calories 257
Fat 8g
Carbs 36g
Fiber 6g
Sugar 5g
Protein 12g

ARTICHOKE AND OLIVE SALAD
Yields: 5 servings

Ingredients

- 1 cup canned artichoke hearts, chopped
- 12 oz. canned chunk light tuna flakes, drained
- 2 tsp. lemon juice
- ⅓ cup low-fat mayonnaise
- ½ cup chopped olives

- ½ tsp. dried oregano

Instructions

1. Put all ingredients in a bowl.
2. Toss to coat.

Nutritional Information per Serving:

Calories 103
Fat 5g
Carbs 8g
Fiber 2g
Sugar 1g
Protein 8g

SAUTEED SQUASH AND GORGONZOLA POLENTA

Yields: 4 servings

Ingredients

- 1 cup water
- 14 oz. canned vegetable stock, divided
- ½ tsp. pepper
- ¾ cup cornmeal
- ⅔ cup Gorgonzola cheese, crumbled
- 3 tbsp. garlic, minced
- 2 tbsp. olive oil
- 1 summer squash, cut into half lengthwise and sliced
- 2 zucchinis, cut into half lengthwise and sliced
- 2 tbsp. flour
- ¼ cup fresh basil, chopped

Instructions

1. Put water and half of the stock in a saucepan and boil.
2. Add pepper and cornmeal.
3. Stir until smooth.
4. Reduce heat and cover.
5. Keep cooking while stirring occasionally.
6. Wait for consistency to become thick.
7. Add gorgonzola.
8. Remove it from heat.
9. In a skillet, heat oil and cook garlic for one minute.
10. Cook squash and zucchini for five minutes.
11. Dust flour on top of the vegetables.
12. Mix to coat.
13. Add remaining stock. Bring to a boil.
14. Simmer and cook for three more minutes.
15. Put the sautéed vegetables on top of the polenta.
16. Sprinkle basil on top before serving.

Nutritional Information per Serving:

Calories 266
Fat 13g
Carbs 30g
Fiber 5g
Sugar 4g
Protein 9g

TOMATO AND CORN SOUP
Yields: 6 servings

Ingredients

- 1 sweet onion, sliced
- 1½ lb. tomatoes, sliced
- 3 cloves garlic, unpeeled
- 1 tbsp. olive oil
- 1 tsp. olive oil
- Salt and pepper to taste
- ¼ tsp. Worcestershire sauce
- 1 tsp. tomato paste
- 2 cups low-sodium chicken stock, divided
- 1 tbsp. basil, chopped
- ½ cup corn kernels

Instructions

1. Preheat your oven to 400°F.
2. Coat your baking pan with cooking spray.
3. In a bowl, pour one tablespoon olive oil.
4. Add onion, garlic and tomatoes.
5. Sprinkle salt and pepper.
6. Toss to coat.
7. Put these on the baking pan and roast for 30 minutes.
8. Remove the seeds from the tomatoes and the ends in the onion.
9. Peel the cloves of garlic.
10. Blend these in a food processor with one cup stock and remaining oil.
11. Pour mixture in a pot.
12. Add remaining stock, tomato paste, tomato juice, basil, brown sugar and Worcestershire sauce.
13. Simmer for a few minutes.
14. Garnish with corn before serving.

Nutritional Information per Serving:
Calories 88

Fat 4g
Carbs 13g
Fiber 3g
Sugar 6g
Protein 3g

SPINACH SALAD WITH TUNA
Yields: 1 serving

Ingredients

- 1½ tbsp. freshly-squeezed lemon juice
- 1½ tbsp. water
- 1½ tbsp. tahini
- 4 pieces Kalamata olives, pitted and chopped
- 5 oz. canned chunk light tuna flakes in water, drained
- 2 cups baby spinach
- 2 tbsp. parsley
- 2 tbsp. feta cheese

Instructions

1. Combine lemon juice, water and tahini in a bowl.
2. Add olives, tuna, feta, and parsley.
3. Pour mixture on top of spinach before serving.

Nutritional Information per Serving:
Calories 375
Fat 21g
Carbs 26g

Fiber 6g
Sugar 14g
Protein 26g

GRILLED CALAMARI WITH VEGGIE SALAD

Yields: 6 servings

Ingredients

- 2½ tbsp. olive oil, divided
- 1 lb. calamari, trimmed, cleaned and sliced
- Salt and pepper to taste
- 1 lb. asparagus, trimmed
- 1 lb. potatoes, quarter cut
- 2 red bell peppers, seeded and sliced
- 1 onion, sliced
- ⅓ cup black olives, pitted and chopped
- ⅓ cup green olives, pitted and chopped
- ¼ cup balsamic vinegar
- ¼ cup fresh basil, chopped
- 2 cloves garlic, minced

Instructions

1. Preheat your grill.
2. Slice the body of the calamari.
3. In a bowl, combine one tablespoon olive oil, salt and pepper.
4. Brush calamari with this mixture.
5. Grill calamari for two minutes and flip.
6. Wait until the calamari becomes opaque.
7. In a pot, cook potatoes for 10 minutes.

8. Remove from water and set aside.
9. Blanch asparagus in water for two minutes.
    10. In a bowl, combine remaining oil, onion, olive, basil, garlic, red pepper, bell pepper and vinegar.
    11. Toss vegetables in this mixture.
    12. Serve with grilled calamari.

Nutritional Information per Serving:

Calories 248
Fat 10g
Carbs 23g
Fiber 4g
Sugar 7g
Protein 16g

FLANK STEAK GYROS

Yields: 4 servings

Ingredients

- ¾ tsp. ground cumin
- ¾ tsp. dried thyme
- ¾ tsp. ground coriander
- 2 tbsp. olive oil, divided
- Salt and pepper to taste
- 1 lb. flank steak, trimmed
- 1 onion, sliced
- 1 cup water
- ½ cup white vinegar
- 1 tsp. white sugar
- 3 cups cucumber, sliced

- 4 whole-wheat pitas, warmed
- ½ cup tzatziki sauce

Instructions

1. Preheat your broiler to high.
2. Line baking pan with a little bit of oil.
3. In a bowl, mix cumin, thyme, coriander, oil, salt and pepper.
4. Brush steak with this oil mixture.
5. Put steak on the baking pan.
6. Top with onion.
7. Broil until steak reaches 145°F or for 15 minutes.
8. In a saucepan, combine water, sugar, salt and vinegar.
9. Bring to a boil.
10. Cook the vegetables for one minute.
11. Remove veggies from heat and strain.
12. Serve with pita bread, steak and tzatziki

Nutritional Information per Serving:

Calories 465
Fat 18g
Carbs 45g
Fiber 7g
Sugar 5g
Protein 33g

SALMON WITH APPLE AND WALNUT SALAD
Yields: 6 servings

Ingredients

Lentil Salad

- 1 cup green lentils
- 6 cups water, divided
- 1 cup dry red wine
- 1 medium onion, cut into half
- 5 cloves garlic, peeled and crushed
- 1 carrot, cut into half
- 3 stems parsley, sliced
- 2 sprigs fresh thyme
- 3 whole cloves
- 1 bay leaf
- 1 tbsp. olive oil
- Salt and pepper to taste
- 2 tbsp. toasted walnuts, chopped
- ½ apple, diced
- 1 tbsp. fresh parsley, chopped

Salmon

- 1 tsp. olive oil
- Salt to taste
- 5 sprigs fresh thyme
- 1½ lbs. salmon fillet, skinned

Instructions

1. In a saucepan, put two cups water and lentils.
2. Bring to a boil and cook for five minutes.
3. Drain and put back into the pan.
4. Add four cups water, onion, garlic, carrot and wine into the pan.
5. Put thyme, cloves, bay leaf and parsley in a cheesecloth.

6. Add this to the pan.
7. Boil and then simmer for 30 minutes.
8. Add salt and pepper to taste.
9. Cook for 20 minutes more.
10. Drain and reserve one cup of the liquid.
11. Discard cheesecloth.
12. Dice the carrots and onions and add to the blender.
13. Add lentils and reserved liquid.
14. Puree until consistency is smooth.
15. Put apple, walnuts and parsley in a bowl and top with the mixture.
16. Brush oil, salt and thyme on both sides of the salmon.
17. Broil for six minutes.
18. Serve with salad.

Nutritional Information per Serving:

Calories 437
Fat 21g
Carbs 25g
Fiber 6g
Sugar 4g
Protein 31g

CHICKEN PESTO AND BEAN SOUP

Yields: 6 servings

Ingredients

- 1 cup onion, chopped
- 2 cloves garlic, minced

- 2 tbsp. olive oil
- 1 tsp. dried marjoram
- 1 tsp. dried oregano
- 2 lb. chicken breasts (skinless)
- 8 cups low-sodium chicken stock
- 3 cups broccolini
- 3 cups fennel, sliced
- 15 oz. canned cannellini beans, rinsed and drained
- 2 cups tomatoes, chopped
- Salt and pepper to taste
- ¼ cup pesto

Instructions

1. Cook onion and garlic in oil for three minutes.
2. Season with marjoram and oregano.
3. Add stock and chicken.
4. Increase heat and bring to a boil.
5. Simmer for 20 minutes.
6. Remove chicken from heat and shred with a fork.
7. In a pot, cook tomatoes, fennel and broccolini for 10 minutes.
8. Add chicken, beans, salt and pepper.
9. Cook for three minutes.
10. Add pesto before serving.

Nutritional Information per Serving:

Calories 264
Fat 11g
Carbs 18g
Fiber 5g
Sugar 4g
Protein 27g

SHRIMP AND BEET SALAD

Yields: 1 serving

Ingredients

- 1 cup watercress
- 1 cup cooked beet, sliced into wedges
- 2 cups arugula
- ½ cup fennel, sliced
- ½ cup zucchini, sliced
- ½ cup barley, cooked
- 4 oz. shrimp, cooked and peeled
- 1 tbsp. red wine vinegar
- 2 tbsp. olive oil
- ½ tsp. shallot, minced
- ½ tsp. Dijon mustard
- Salt and pepper to taste

Instructions

1. Put beets, watercress, fennel, barley, zucchini, shrimp and arugula on a serving platter.
2. In a bowl, mix vinegar, mustard, oil, salt, pepper and shallots.
3. Pour over the salad.

Nutritional Information per Serving:

Calories 584
Fat 30g
Carbs 47g
Fiber 9g
Sugar 12g
Protein 35g

SPANISH MUSSELS

Yields: 2 servings

Ingredients

- 2 tsp. olive oil
- 2 cloves garlic, minced
- 1 onion, chopped
- 8 cherry tomatoes, cut into half
- 8 oz. canned chickpeas, rinsed and drained
- 4 oz. pimientos, rinsed and chopped
- Pinch of saffron
- 2 tsp. oregano, chopped
- ½ tsp. freshly-ground pepper
- ½ cup vegetable broth
- ¼ cup dry sherry
- 2 lb. mussels, scrubbed and beard removed

Instructions

1. In a pan over medium heat, pour olive oil and cook garlic, onion, tomatoes, chickpeas and pimientos for six minutes.
2. Add saffron, oregano and pepper.
3. Cook for 30 seconds.
4. Pour in the vegetable stock.
5. Simmer for 15 minutes.
6. Add the mussels and simmer for eight minutes.
7. Discard any mussels that did not open.

Nutritional Information per Serving:

Calories 368
Fat 10g
Carbs 38g

Fiber 7g
Sugar 5g
Protein 27g

Yields: 4 servings

Ingredients

- 4 tbsp. olive oil, divided
- 2 tbsp. lemon juice
- 1 tsp. lemon zest
- ½ tsp. salt, divided
- ½ tsp. pepper, divided
- 1 tsp. dried oregano
- 14 pieces extra firm tofu, drained and cubed
- 16 cherry tomatoes
- 1 eggplant, sliced
- 1 zucchini, sliced
- 1 yellow bell pepper, sliced
- 1 onion, cut into half
- 2 tbsp. tomato paste

Instructions

1. In a bowl, combine one tablespoon olive oil, lemon juice and lemon zest.
2. Add half of salt and pepper, and oregano.
3. Marinate tofu in the mixture.
4. Preheat the grill.
5. In another bowl, toss vegetables in remaining oil, tomato paste, salt and pepper.

6. Add tofu and vegetables to the skewers.
7. Brush with the marinade.
8. Grill for three to five minutes.

Nutritional Information per Serving:

Calories 252
Fat 19g
Carbs 14g
Fiber 4g
Sugar 8g
Protein 11g

PORK TENDERLOIN

Yields: 4 servings

Ingredients

- 1 tsp. salt
- 1 tsp. pepper
- 2 tsp. fresh sage, chopped
- 1 tsp. fresh rosemary, chopped
- 1 tsp. garlic, minced
- 4 pork tenderloins, sliced thinly
- 4 slices ham
- 1 cup Parmesan cheese, grated
- 3 tsp. olive oil, divided

Instructions

1. Put salt, pepper, sage, rosemary and garlic in a bowl. Mix well.

2. Preheat your oven to 450°F.
3. Rub herb mixture on both sides of pork tenderloin.
4. Put a slice of ham on each slice of pork tenderloin.
5. Top with cheese.
6. Drizzle olive oil all over.
7. Roll the pork tenderloin and secure with a toothpick.
8. Bake in the oven until cooked through.

Nutritional Information per Serving:

Calories 175
Fat 7g
Carbs 1g
Fiber 0g
Sugar 0g
Protein 26g

15 RECIPES FOR DESSERTS AND SNACKS
APRICOT JAM TART

Yields: 8 servings

Ingredients

- ⅔ lb. low-fat butter
- 1 lb. whole-wheat flour
- ¾ cup sugar
- 2 eggs
- 2 tsp. baking powder
- ⅔ lb. apricot jam

Instructions

1. Beat butter, sugar and egg.
2. Slowly add the flour and mix until well blended.
3. Refrigerate the dough for 30 minutes.
4. Coat a tart pan with butter.
5. Divide the dough into three.
6. Then combine two of the portions, and roll it out into the pan.
7. Make sure that the dough reaches the raised sides of the tart pan.
8. Spread a thick even layer of the jam onto the dough.
9. Roll out the remaining dough.
10. Slice into strips.
11. Put these strips on top of the jam.
12. Bake the tart in the oven at 350°F for 45 minutes.

Nutritional Information per Serving:

Calories 357
Fat 21.5g
Carbs 43.6g
Sugar 35.1g
Fiber 1.8g
Protein 8.9g

CHOCOLATE BROWNIES
Yields: 16 servings

Ingredients

- ½ cup unsweetened cocoa powder
- ¾ cup whole-wheat flour
- ¼ tsp. baking soda

- ½ tsp. salt
- ½ cup unsweetened applesauce
- ½ cup plain Greek yogurt
- 1 cup brown sugar
- 2 eggs
- 2 tbsp. oil
- 2 oz. semisweet chocolate, melted
- 2 oz. semisweet chocolate, chopped

Instructions

1. Preheat your oven to 350°F.
2. Coat square baking pan with cooking spray.
3. Line it with parchment paper.
4. In a mixing bowl, combine cocoa, flour, baking soda and salt.
5. In another bowl, mix applesauce, yogurt, eggs, oil sugar and melted chocolate.
6. Once blended, slowly add flour mixture.
7. Stir.
8. Pour batter and spread into the baking pan.
9. Top with chopped chocolate.
10. Bake in the oven for 30 to 35 minutes.

Nutritional Information per Serving:

Calories 139
Fat 4.8g
Carbs 23g
Fiber 0g
Sugar 17g
Protein 2.8g

PLUM CAKES

Yields: 12 servings

Ingredients

- ¼ flaxseed meal
- ¾ cup whole-wheat flour
- ¼ tsp. salt
- 1½ tsp. baking powder
- 3 tbsp. unsalted butter
- 2 tbsp. avocado
- 1 egg
- ⅓ cup sugar
- 1 tsp. lemon zest, grated
- ⅔ cup low-fat milk
- 1 tsp. vanilla extract
- 1 plum, pitted and sliced thinly

Instructions

1. Preheat your oven to 350°F.
2. Coat muffin pan with cooking spray.
3. In a bowl, combine flaxseed meal, flour, salt and baking powder.
4. In the electric mixer, beat sugar, avocado and butter until the consistency becomes fluffy.
5. Add lemon zest, vanilla and egg.
6. Beat and mix well.
7. Turn mixer speed to low and add the dry mixture alternating with the milk.
8. Pour batter into the muffin cup.
9. Put plum slices on top.
10. Bake in the oven for 20 to 25 minutes.

Nutritional Information per Serving:
Calories 113
Fat 5g
Carbs 14g
Fiber 1g
Sugar 20g
Protein 0g

YOGURT POPSICLE
Yields: 6 servings

Ingredients

- 1 cup frozen strawberries
- 1 cup frozen blueberries
- 4 tbsp. Greek yogurt
- 2 tbsp. honey

Instructions

1. Mix berries, yogurt and honey in the blender.
2. Blend until consistency becomes smooth.
3. Put mixture into the cups.
4. Freeze until mixture hardens.

Nutritional Information per Serving:
Calories 44
Fat 0.3g
Carbs 10.2g
Fiber 1g

Sugar 8.8g
Protein 0.9g

WATERMELON SORBET

Yields: 10 servings

Ingredients

- ⅔ cup sugar
- ¾ cup water
- 3 tbsp. freshly-squeezed lime juice
- 6 cups watermelon, seeded and sliced

Instructions

1. Put sugar and water in a saucepan.
2. Turn heat to medium high.
3. Bring to a boil.
4. Reduce heat and simmer for six to seven minutes.
5. Remove from the stove.
6. Let cool in room temperature.
7. Cover with foil and then chill in the refrigerator for one hour.
8. Put lime juice and watermelon in a food processor.
9. Pulse until the consistency becomes smooth.
10. Add the chilled sugar mixture.
11. Put in a baking dish and freeze for half an hour.
12. Serve immediately.

Nutritional Information per Serving:

Calories 77
Fat 0.1g

Carbs 20.2g
Fiber 0g
Sugar 18.9g
Protein 0.5g

PEARS IN WINE

Yields: 6 servings

Ingredients

- 6 pears, peeled but stem left intact
- 3 cups red wine
- 4 oz. sugar
- 6 cloves cinnamon
- 1 stick cinnamon

Instructions

1. Let the pears stand in an upright position in your pan.
2. Pour the wine over the pears.
3. Sprinkle with sugar.
4. Simmer for 20 minutes.
5. Add cinnamon cloves and stick.
6. Simmer for another 20 minutes.
7. Turn off the heat and let cool.
8. Pour remaining wine sauce over the pears before serving.

Nutritional Information per Serving:

Calories 287
Fat 0.3g
Carbs 25.9g
Fiber 6.5g
Sugar 38g
Protein 0.8g

YOGURT AND FRUITS

Yields: 6 servings

Ingredients

- 4 oz. strawberries
- 5 oz. raspberries
- 3 tbsp. red wine
- 4 tbsp. sugar
- 1¼ cups Greek yogurt
- 1¼ cups fresh low-fat cream
- 1 tsp. mint leaves

Instructions

1. Put the berries in a bowl.
2. Sprinkle sugar on top of the berries.
3. Pour wine.
4. Toss to coat.
5. Let berries sit for a few minutes.
6. Whip fresh cream in a bowl until you see soft peaks forming.
7. Add yogurt. Mix well.
8. Fold the cream and yogurt mixture into the berry mixture.
9. Pour mixture into a serving cup.
10. Top with mint leaves.

Nutritional Information per Serving:

Calories 55
Fat 0.2g
Carbs 12.5g
Fiber 2g

Sugar 10g
Protein 0.4g

YOGURT MOUSSE WITH CHERRY PRESERVE

Yields: 4 servings

Ingredients

- 1 tbsp. unflavored gelatin
- ¼ cup cold water
- ⅓ cup sugar
- ½ tsp. vanilla extract
- 2 cups sour cherries, pureed
- 1 pot plain yogurt
- 1 cup chilled heavy cream

Instructions

1. Sprinkle unflavored gelatin into a saucepan filled with cold water. Mix.
2. Wait for one minute and then simmer the mixture until the gelatin dissolves.
3. In a bowl, mix sugar, vanilla and sour cherry puree.
4. Add in the gelatin mixture.
5. Add the yogurt.
6. Beat cream until there are stiff peaks forming.
7. Fold cream into the mixture.
8. Pour mixture into dessert glasses.

Nutritional Information per Serving:

Calories 64
Fat 0g
Carbs 16.7g
Fiber 0g
Sugar 16.7g
Protein 0g

CHICKEN PARMESAN SANDWICH
Yields: 2 servings

Ingredients

- ¼ tsp. salt
- ½ tsp. pepper
- ¼ cup all-purpose flour
- 2 chicken breasts (boneless, skinless, fat trimmed)
- 3 tsp. olive oil, divided
- ⅓ cup marinara sauce
- 6 oz. spinach
- ¼ cup mozzarella cheese, shredded
- 2 tbsp. Parmesan cheese, grated
- 2 whole-wheat sandwich rolls, toasted

Instructions

1. In a platter, mix salt, pepper and flour.
2. Put chicken in between plastic sheets and pound with a meat mallet.
3. Dredge it in the flour mixture.
4. In a pan over medium heat, pour a little oil and cook spinach for two minutes.
5. Remove from the pan and set aside.
6. Pour oil into the pan and cook chicken for two to three minutes.
7. Top chicken with spinach, marinara sauce and Parmesan cheese.
8. Sprinkle mozzarella cheese on top.
9. Cover and wait until chicken is cooked thoroughly and cheese has melted.
   10. Serve with rolls.

Nutritional Information per Serving:

Calories 468
Fat 16g
Carbs 45g
Fiber 4g
Sugar 5g
Protein 38g

TURKEY PANINI
Yields: 4 servings

Ingredients

- 2 tbsp. low-fat plain yogurt
- 3 tbsp. low-fat mayonnaise
- 2 tbsp. fresh basil, chopped
- 2 tbsp. Parmesan cheese, shredded
- 1 tsp. lemon juice
- Salt and pepper to taste
- 8 oz. low-sodium deli turkey
- 8 slices tomato
- 8 slices whole-wheat bread
- 2 tsp. olive oil

Instructions

1. In a bowl, mix yogurt, mayo, basil, Parmesan, pepper and lemon juice.
2. Spread mixture evenly on bread slices.
3. Put turkey and tomato slices on the bread.
4. Top with the other bread slice.

5. Heat oil in the pan and toast panini until golden.
6. Flip and do the same for the other side.

Nutritional Information per Serving:

Calories 314
Fat 8g
Carbs 37g
Fiber 5g
Sugar 6g
Protein 22g

MOZZARELLA AND TOMATO SANDWICHES
Yields: 4 servings

Ingredients

- ⅓ cup sun-dried tomatoes
- 1 bowl water
- 1 clove garlic, peeled and crushed
- ¼ tsp. salt
- ⅛ tsp. red pepper, crushed
- 1 tbsp. freshly-squeezed lemon juice
- 2 tbsp. olive oil
- ¼ cup olives, chopped
- 8 slices whole-grain sourdough bread
- 4 oz. fresh mozzarella, sliced
- Salt and pepper to taste
- 3 tomatoes, sliced
- 2 tsp. balsamic vinegar
- 1 cup fresh basil leaves

Instructions

1. Pour boiling water in a bowl.
2. Add sun-dried tomatoes.
3. Let sit for 10 minutes.
4. Mash garlic and salt until consistency becomes similar to a paste.
5. Put this in a bowl and add red pepper, lemon juice and half of the olive oil.
6. Drain tomatoes and chop finely.
7. Add chopped tomatoes and olives to the dressing.
8. Spread a layer of this mixture on the bread slice.
9. Top with cheese, tomato slices, pepper, salt and vinegar.
10. Top with basil before putting the other bread slice on top.
11. Repeat procedure for the other sandwiches.

Nutritional Information per Serving:
Calories 385
Fat 18g
Carbs 39g
Fiber 6g
Sugar 9g
Protein 14g

VEGETARIAN FINGER SANDWICHES
Yields: 4 servings

Ingredients

- 4 slices whole-wheat bread
- 8 tsp. low-fat mayonnaise, divided
- 4 tsp. fresh basil, chopped
- 1 tomato, sliced
- Salt and pepper to taste

Instructions

1. Use a round cookie cutter to cut bread into circles.
2. Spread mayo on each slice.
3. Top with basil and tomatoes.
4. Season with salt and pepper.

Nutritional Information per Serving:

Calories 85
Fat 3g
Carbs 13g
Fiber 2g
Sugar 2g
Protein 3g

VEGETABLE PIZZA

Yields: 4 servings

Ingredients

- 1 lb. whole-wheat pizza dough
- 2 tbsp. olive oil, divided
- 1 eggplant, sliced
- Salt and pepper to taste
- ⅓ cup feta cheese, crumbled

- 2 tomatoes, chopped
- 4 tbsp. fresh mint, chopped

Instructions

1. Preheat your oven to 350°F.
2. In a bowl, coat eggplant with half of the olive oil.
3. Season with salt and pepper.
4. Grill eggplant and chop.
5. Combine tomatoes, feta cheese, and eggplant.
6. Add half of the mint and the remaining oil.
7. Season with salt and pepper.
8. Roll out the pizza dough.
9. Spread eggplant mixture on top of the pizza.
10. Bake pizza in the oven until crust is golden brown.
11. Top with remaining mint before serving.

Nutritional Information per Serving:

Calories 336
Fat 13g
Carbs 47g
Fiber 9g
Sugar 7g
Protein 10g

DOLMA WRAP
Yields: 1 serving

Ingredients

- ¼ cup cucumber, chopped
- ½ cup Romaine lettuce, shredded

- ¼ cup tomato, chopped
- ⅛ tsp. garlic powder
- 1 tbsp. feta cheese, crumbled
- ¼ cup reduced-fat plain yogurt
- 1 whole-wheat wrap
- 3 prepared dolmas

Instructions

1. Put cucumber, Romaine lettuce, tomato, garlic powder and feta cheese in a bowl.
2. Mix well.
3. Spread a layer on the whole-wheat wrap.
4. Top with the dolmas before rolling the wrap.

Nutritional Information per Serving:

Calories 384
Fat 4g
Carbs 66g
Fiber 9g
Sugar 10g
Protein 15g

WHITE BEAN SPREAD ON CRACKERS

Yields: 1 serving

Ingredients

- 1 tbsp. feta cheese
- ½ cup canned white beans, rinsed and drained

- 2 tsp. vinaigrette
- 3 crackers
- ⅔ cup carrots, shredded
- 1 tbsp. freshly-squeezed lemon juice

Instructions

1. Mash feta, white beans and vinaigrette in a bowl.
2. Spread mixture evenly on the crackers.
3. Toss shredded carrots in lemon juice.
4. Top crackers with carrots before serving.

Nutritional Information per Serving:

Calories 325

Fat 14g

Carbs 49g

Fiber 8g

Sugar 5g

Protein 9g

KICKSTART YOUR DAY BERRY SMOOTHIE

(Prep: 5 minutes. Calories: 100)

Ingredients

- 1 juicy peach
- ½ cup Greek yogurt or plain yogurt
- 1 small banana, peeled
- ⅔ cup hulled strawberries
- 1 tsp flaxseeds

Method

- Cut the peach in half, remove the pit and cube the pulp.
- Add all ingredients to a food processor.
- Blitz until the ingredients are combined.
- Serve immediately, or chill for an hour before serving.

YOGURT BOWL

Prep time: 5 minutes. Calories: 364. Protein: 24g)

Ingredients

- 1 cup plain Greek yogurt
- ½ banana sliced
- 3 strawberries hulled and sliced
- ¼ cup fresh blueberries
- 2 tbsp raw local organic honey.

Method

- In a bowl, place the yogurt.
- Add the sliced banana and berries.
- Drizzle honey on top.
- Serve chilled.

Tip: Make the breakfast bowl more nutritious by sprinkling seeds and nuts on it.

Mediterranean Omelet

(Prep time: 10 minutes. Calories: 560. Protein: 20g)

This omelet is packed with protein and vegetables.

Ingredients

- 2 large eggs
- 2 tbsp extra virgin olive oil
- 1 medium yellow onion chopped
- 1 clove garlic minced
- 1 cup spinach chopped
- ½ medium tomato diced
- 2 tbsp skim milk
- 4 kalamata olives pitted and diced
- Salt and pepper to taste
- 3 tbsp crumbled feta cheese
- 1 tbsp chopped fresh parsley

Method

- In a frying pan, heat the oil.
- Add onions and fry till browned. Also add garlic and fry for 2 minutes.
- Add the salt, spinach and tomatoes and cook for a few minutes.
- In a bowl, whisk together egg and milk.
- Add pepper and olives to the pan and pour the egg mixture over the sautéed vegetables.
- Spread around and turn the heat up so the egg cooks quickly. You can lift the omelet a bit to allow the upper liquid layer to go underneath the cooked egg. Continue cooking till the egg is cooked.
- Fold the omelet in half. Slide onto a plate and add cheese and freshly chopped parsley. Serve warm.

4. Buckwheat Pancakes

(Prep time: 20 minutes. Calories: 240. Protein: 11g. Fiber: 12g)

Buckwheat is a cereal grain and one of the healthiest foods you can have for breakfast.

Ingredients

- 1 egg
- ¼ tsp baking soda
- 1 tsp baking powder
- 1 ¼ cup buttermilk
- 1 cup buckwheat flour
- 1 ½ tsp Stevia sweetener
- ¼ tsp vanilla extract

• Pinch of salt
• 1 tbsp clarified butter (also called ghee, this is much healthier than regular butter. You can make it at home by boiling regular unsalted butter till the whey separates, and you are left with clear brown liquid on top). You can also use regular butter.

Method

• In a bowl, mix together buckwheat flour, soda, baking powder, sweetener and salt.
• In another bowl, mix all wet ingredients: buttermilk, extract, and egg. Whisk together.
• Mix the dry and wet ingredients to form a thick, smooth batter. Let it rest for 15 minutes.
• Heat a skillet and add some clarified ghee or butter.
• Pour a large spoonful of batter in the center of the skillet a few inches in diameter and less than an inch in thickness. Let the batter bubble over which indicates it is time to flip it.
• Flip the pancake and cook on both sides, pouring some more butter or ghee if needed to prevent sticking. Pancake is done once it is brown, in about 2-3 minutes.
• Repeat these steps for the remaining batter.
• Serve the pancakes warm with maple syrup, fruit or honey.

5. Breakfast Couscous

(Prep time: 18 minutes. Calories: 259. Protein: 13g)

Couscous is a popular alternative to rice and pasta, and you can have it for breakfast without piling on too many calories to your daily allowance.

Ingredients

- 1 cup uncooked whole wheat couscous
- 3 cups skim milk
- One 2" cinnamon stick
- 6 tsp brown sugar divided
- Pinch of salt
- 4 tsp butter divided
- ¼ cup raisins and currants
- ½ cup dried apricots

Method

- In a medium pan, combine milk and cinnamon and boil for 3 minutes, stirring continuously.
- Remove from heat; add the dried fruits, couscous, currants and salt and 4 tsp of brown sugar to the pan. Mix well. Cover and keep aside for 15 minutes.
- Pour into 4 serving bowls and add 1 tsp butter and ½ tsp brown sugar on top of each bowl. Stir and serve immediately.

6. Simple Mediterranean Breakfast a la Roma
(Prep time: 10 minutes. Calories: 425. Protein: 12g)
This is a simple Roman breakfast eaten in the summer, when the tomatoes are full of rich flavors.
Ingredients
- 50g fresh ricotta cheese
- 2 boiled or poached eggs
- 1 slice sourdough rye bread
- 2-3 slices of fresh Roma tomatoes
- 1-2 tsp olive oil
- Sea salt and fresh black pepper to taste

Method

- Spread the ricotta on the bread, top with eggs. On the plate, place the assembled bread next to tomato wedges. Drizzle olive oil and season with salt and pepper.

7. Oatmeal With Fruits And Nuts

(Prep time: 5 minutes. Calories: 150 with water, or 230 if you use skim milk.)

Breakfast cannot get any simpler than this.

Ingredients

- ½ cup oats (will cook to 1 cup)
- 1 cup skim milk or water
- ¼ tsp cinnamon
- 1 chopped apple
- Handful of raisins
- ¼ cup dried cranberries
- Assorted nuts, blanched and slivered to sprinkle on top
- ½ tsp brown sugar, molasses, Stevia or honey (optional)

Method

- Cook the oats as per instructions, and add remaining ingredients.
- Add seasonal fruits and nuts to enhance the flavor of the oatmeal. You can add blueberries, strawberries and maple syrup for a classic combination.

8.Fruit And Yogurt Parfait With Granola

(Prep time: 5 minutes. Calories: 200.)

Another simple breakfast for the weight watchers on the Med diet, this is a quick and easy recipe that is tasty, healthy and crunchy.

Ingredients

- 1 cup low fat plain Greek yogurt
- 1 tsp honey
- ¼ cup granola cereal
- Fresh or frozen fruits

Method

- Mix yogurt and honey. Add the fruit and sprinkle granola on top.

Tip: Do not stir the granola into the mixture to keep it crispy.

9. Italian Omelet

(Prep time: 25 minutes. Calories: 450)

This is a delicious breakfast served in Italy.

Ingredients

- 1 cup sliced mushrooms and zucchini
- 3 tbsp olive oil divided
- 4 eggs
- 3 tbsp water
- Salt and pepper
- ½ cup mozzarella
- For the sauce: 1 tbsp olive oil, 1 chopped medium tomato, 2 tbsp chopped parsley, 1 clove garlic, ½ tsp basil, pinch of salt.

Method

- In a skillet, heat some olive oil and add the zucchini and mushrooms. Sauté until brown. Keep them aside (warm).
- In a bowl, whisk together eggs, water, salt and pepper. Heat the skillet and add remaining oil. Add the beaten eggs. Cook for a few minutes. As the eggs cook, push the uncooked portion beneath, and let the top part set. One the eggs are cooked, add the vegetables over one side and sprinkle mozzarella cheese. Fold the other half of the egg over the filling. Remove the eggs on a plate.
- To make the sauce, heat the oil. Add tomatoes, garlic, basil and parsley. Cook until heated through.
- Serve the sauce with the omelet.

10. Healthy Porridge With Rolled Oats

(Prep time: 5 minutes. Calories: 223)

This porridge contains oats and yogurt. It is a cold porridge that is great for breakfast or for an afternoon snack. Make a larger batch and store the porridge in the fridge for up to 4 days.

Ingredients

- 1 cup low fat plain yogurt mixed with ½ 1bsp. honey, or 1 cup vanilla flavored yogurt
- ¼ cup rolled oats
- 1 tbsp rye flakes
- Plums, sliced bananas, ground cinnamon and some more yogurt to serve.

Method

• Mix oats and rye flakes with yogurt and let stand overnight in the refrigerator.
• In the morning, serve with plums, cinnamon, bananas and yogurt and drizzle some more honey on top.

Did you know that the Med diet is also called the "anti-cancer diet?"[11] In this chapter, we will be covering easy lunch recipes that won't take too much of your time and will provide an abundant supply of antioxidants. The main ingredients are healthy grains, seasonal vegetables, and lean meat. Enjoy!

1. Polenta

(Prep time: 15 minutes. Calories: 112. Protein: 5g)

Serve this polenta dish with your favorite bread or soup, or enjoy it alone.

Ingredients

- ½ cup cornmeal or yellow polenta
- 1 cup skim milk
- 2 cups homemade stock or water
- 1 cup cheese
- 1-2 tbsp butter (optional)

Method

- Bring water/stock and milk to a boil.
- Add the polenta and whisk. Stir continuously.
- Polenta will take about 10 minutes to cook. The consistency should resemble mashed potatoes.
- Remove from heat. Add cheese.
- Cover and keep for 5 minutes.
- Serve warm.

2. Moroccan Chickpea Soup

(Prep time: 20 minutes. Calories: 107)

This is a hearty soup recipe perfect for cold days. You can make a large batch and keep it in the refrigerator for up to 3 days. Pack it in an airtight container and take it to work.

Ingredients

- 2 tsp olive oil
- 1 medium onion, chopped
- 2 medium carrots, diced
- 2 celery sticks, cleaned and diced
- 2 cans of chickpeas rinsed
- 1 can of low sodium tomatoes
- 2 crushed garlic cloves
- 2 tsp Moroccan seasoning

- 2 cups low sodium vegetable or chicken stock
- 1 cup water
- Fresh coriander leaves, chopped (optional)
- Fresh low fat yogurt (optional)
- Black pepper to taste

Method

- In a large saucepan, heat the oil and add the chopped veggies. Cover and cook for 3 minutes until vegetables are soft.
- Add garlic and fry for a minute.
- Add the chickpeas, tomatoes, stock and water. Bring the mixture to a boil, then cover and simmer for up to 10 minutes.
- Remove half the soup in a bowl and cool. Pour this half in a blender and blend until creamy. Return the creamy soup to the remaining soup in the pan. Heat over medium heat for 2-3 minutes.
- Ladle into bowls and serve with yogurt (optional), and garnish with freshly chopped cilantro or coriander leaves.

3. Bean And Salmon Stir Fry

(Prep time: 10 minutes. Calories: 127)

Seafood and Chinese food lovers will love this bean and salmon stir fry recipe. Serve with brown rice for a filling and healthy meal.

Ingredients

- ¼ cup water
- 2 tbsp each rice vinegar and black bean garlic sauce.
- 1 tbsp dry sherry
- 2 tbsp cornflour
- 1 tbsp olive oil
- 500g salmon chopped into small cubes
- 2 cups mung sprouts
- 1 bunch sliced scallions.

Method

- In a small bowl, mix water, cornflour, vinegar, bean garlic sauce and sherry.
- In a large skillet, heat the oil and add the salmon cubes. Fry the pieces until browned. Add the mung bean sprouts, scallions and the bean garlic sauce mixture. Stir to coat the salmon pieces.
- Cook for 2-3 minutes until the sprouts are tender.
- Serve with sautéed veggies or brown rice.

4. Easy Red Cabbage And Walnut Slaw

(Prep time: 10 minutes. Calories: 150)

This delicious, light slaw is an ideal alternative to traditional coleslaw.

Ingredients

- ½ red cabbage sliced thin
- 1 large apple, cored, peeled and grated
- 1 finely chopped shallot
- 2 tbsp apple cider vinegar or red wine vinegar
- 2 tbsp raisins
- Handful of walnuts, chopped
- 2 tbsp each walnut oil and olive oil
- Salt and pepper to taste
- Cilantro sprigs (optional)

Method

• In a bowl, mix the shallot and vinegar and allow the mixture to infuse for 5 minutes.
• Add the oils, seasonings and cabbage. Mix together.
• Add the grated apple and combine.
• Add the raisins and nuts and mix well. You can allow the salad to rest for half an hour or eat immediately. Garnish with cilantro.
• Variation: Add finely chopped tomatoes in place of apple as shown in image above.

5. Easy Shrimp & Chicken Paella

(Prep time: 30 minutes. Calories: 332)

Paella is a Spanish rice dish with chicken or seafood. Your family will love its distinctive flavor and bright colors. The best part is that this dish contains turmeric, an extremely healthy spice with anti-cancer[12] properties.

Ingredients

- 1 tbsp olive oil
- 1 chopped onion
- 2 red bell peppers, sliced
- 6 oz chicken sausages, cubed
- 0.5 lb chicken breasts, cubed
- 3 cups cooked brown rice
- 1 ½ cups frozen peas (thawed)
- 3 garlic cloves crushed
- 3 tsp lemon juice
- 2 tsp each turmeric and coriander powders
- 12 oz small frozen shrimp, peeled

Method

- In a skillet, heat the oil and add onions, peppers, chicken breast cubes and sausage. Fry for a minute then cover and cook for 3-4 minutes until the sausage and chicken breast is cooked thoroughly.
- In a bowl, add rice, lemon juice, peas, garlic, turmeric and coriander powders. Mix well.
- Add the rice mixture to the skillet with chicken. Place the shrimp on top of the rice and cover and cook on low heat until shrimp are cooked through, about 3 minutes.

6. Colorful Vegetable Lentil Medley

(Prep time: 25 minutes. Calories: 300. Protein: 22g)

This is a vegetarian dish with lentils and nutritious veggies. It's a delicious, high-protein recipe that still has very few calories.

Ingredients

- 2 cups vegetable broth
- 1 cup water
- 1 cup lentils, washed
- 3-4 cloves of garlic, crushed
- A pinch of salt, pepper and oregano each
- 6 cups veggies — cubed, sliced or chopped: broccoli, bell peppers, carrots, squash and onions
- 2 tbsp finely chopped mint
- 2 oz crumbled goat cheese
- For the dressing: 1 tbsp Dijon mustard, 2 tbsp olive oil, 1 tsp lemon juice

Method

- In a large pot, heat the stock and water. Add the lentils, salt, pepper, garlic, and oregano and bring to a boil. Reduce heat and simmer for 20 minutes.
- In a steamer, cook all vegetables until tender with a bit of crunch.
- Whisk together the ingredients for the dressing.
- In a large bowl, place the cooked lentils, vegetables, and dressing. Toss until coated.
- Add the crumbled cheese on top and serve.

7. Greek Plaki (Fishy Vegetable Bake)

(Prep time: 30 minutes. Calories: 430)

This is a classic Greek dish that can be eaten hot or cold.

Ingredients

- 3 tbsp olive oil
- 2 medium onions, chopped
- 2 cloves garlic, crushed
- 1 celery stick, cubed
- 2 carrots, sliced
- ¼ cup vegetable stock or water
- ¼ cup white wine
- 2 tomatoes chopped

- 600g firm fish (like cod) cut into steaks or fillet
- 10-12 olives, chopped
- 3 slices of lemon
- Salt, pepper and oregano

Method

- Preheat oven to 350 degrees.
- In a pan, soften onions in olive oil for a few minutes. Add garlic, vegetables, water/stock and wine. Simmer for 5-7 minutes until vegetables are tender. Add tomatoes and oregano and cook for 2-3 minutes more.
- In an oven proof dish, lay the fillets and pour the sauce over them. Scatter the olives over them and add three lemon slices evenly. Cover with an aluminum foil and bake 20 minutes or until the fish flakes when prodded with knife.
- Cool for at least five minutes before serving.

8. Easy Sicilian Eggplant Caponata (Stew)

(Prep time: 30 minutes. Calories: 110)

This dish has a variety of flavors and textures. It has soft eggplant, fragrant and crunchy pine nuts, and fruity tomatoes accompanied by earthy basil. Serve it with brown rice.

Ingredients

- 2 eggplants, diced
- 1 medium onion, sliced
- 4 celery sticks, sliced
- 4-5 tomatoes, chopped
- 4 tbsp olive oil
- 12 black olives, chopped

- 2 tbsp red wine vinegar
- 1 tbsp acacia honey
- 2 tbsp basil or parsley, chopped
- 2 tbsp roasted pine nuts, crushed
- 2 tbsp capers
- Salt and pepper

Method

- Heat olive oil in a heavy bottomed skillet. Add onions and brown them.
- Add celery and eggplants and cook for 10 minutes, stirring occasionally to prevent the vegetables from sticking to the bottom or burning.
- Add tomatoes, honey, capers, olives, and wine vinegar. Cover and cook for 10-12 minutes.
- Before serving, add the parsley or basil and chopped nuts.

9. Grilled Salmon With Herbs

(Prep time: 30 minutes. Calories: 367)

Ingredients

- 450g salmon fillet
- 2 lemon slices
- 20-30 sprigs of fresh herbs like rosemary, thyme, sage, parsley, etc. chopped and divided into 2 batches
- 1 clove garlic, crushed
- 1 tbsp Dijon mustard

Method

- Fire the grill to medium high.
- On a rimless baking sheet, add two layers of heavy duty aluminium foil. Arrange lemon slices in the center of the foil. Add the sprigs of herbs on the slices.
- Crush the garlic with salt. Mix the paste of garlic and salt with 2 tbsp of chopped herbs.
- Spread the mixture on both sides of the fillets.
- Place the salmon over the herb stack. Pick up the foil off the baking sheet and slide it on the grill keeping the salmon, lemon and herbs intact.
- Close the grill and grill the fish on medium high for 18-20 minutes.
- Serve with rice, seasonal grilled vegetables or roasted baby potatoes.

10. Chicken Scaloppine With Lemon Basil Sauce

(Prep time: 20 minutes. Calories: 180)

Don't let the name of this dish intimidate you — it's less complicated than it sounds!

Ingredients

- 1 tbsp olive oil
- ½ cup dry white wine
- ½ cup low sodium chicken broth
- 4 chicken breasts (pound them first to flatten)
- 2 tbsp each lemon juice and capers, drained
- ½ tsp each Worcestershire sauce and ground pepper
- ½ cup parsley chopped

Method

- Heat oil in a non-stick skillet and add wine and broth. Bring to a boil.
- Add chicken and cover. Cook for about 6-8 minutes.
- Remove the chicken from the skillet and keep it covered.
- Continue cooking the leftover sauce in the skillet. Add lemon juice, capers, Worcestershire sauce and pepper. Return the chicken to the sauce and add parsley. Heat through.
- Variation: Add an assortment of colorful vegetables to this recipe to get antioxidants and phytochemicals. Serve as is or with brown rice.

11. Corn Ham Risotto

(Prep time: 30 minutes. Calories: 584)

Ingredients
- 2 tbsp olive oil
- 2 cloves of garlic, crushed
- 1 chopped shallot
- 1 ½ cup Arborio rice
- Salt and pepper to taste
- ¾ cup dry white wine
- 4 cups stock (chicken or vegetable) or water
- 2 cups corn kernels
- 8 oz shredded smoked ham
- 4 oz cheese
- ½ cup chives, chopped (leave some for garnish)

Method

• In a large sauce pan, heat the oil. Add garlic and shallots. Cook for several minutes.
• Add the rice and fry briefly.
• Add wine and stir. Cook for 1-2 minutes until liquid is absorbed.
• Season with salt and pepper.
• Add stock little at a time and cook for 5 minutes. If the rice appears dry, add remaining stock.
• Add the corn and cook until corn becomes tender. Then, add the ham.
• Stir in the cheese until melted.
• Add chives. Add salt and pepper to taste.
• Serve with more cheese and chives on top.

12. Pasta With Zucchini And Smoked Mozzarella

(Prep time: 30 minutes. Calories: 500)

Ingredients
- 2 tbsp butter
- 2 tbsp extra virgin olive oil
- 3 thinly sliced bell pepper
- 1 sliced onion
- 2 medium zucchini cut into ½" slices
- Salt and pepper to taste
- 12 oz pasta of your choice
- 4 oz smoked mozzarella
- ½ cup chopped basil divided for garnish

Method
- Cook pasta according to package instruction. Drain but reserve one cup water.

• In the meanwhile, heat a large sauce pan. Add oil and butter.
• Fry onions, pepper and zucchini until onions and peppers are softened and zucchini is crispy.
• Add the cheese, pasta and one cup of cooking water. Toss to coat the pasta well. Add basil and mix well.
• Add salt and pepper.
• If pasta looks dry, add some water to increase sauce.
• Serve hot, garnished with some more cheese and basil leaves.

13. Flavorful Linguine With Brussels Sprouts
(Prep time: 30 minutes. Calories: 407)
Ingredients
- 1 box linguine
- 2 tbsp olive oil
- Salt and pepper to taste
- 6 slices thick-cut pancetta or bacon
- 1 chopped medium onion
- 1 lb brussel sprouts
- 2 cloves garlic
- 3 oz cheese (parmesan or mozzarella)
- ⅓ cup dry white wine

Method
- Cook the pasta according to box instructions. Drain and set aside. Reserve one cup of cooking water.
- In a pan, heat the oil. Add garlic and onions. Fry until the onions are brown.
- Add the brussel sprouts and sauté until the sprouts turn bright green.
- Add the wine and stir until the liquid is absorbed.
- Add pasta, cheese, cooking water, salt and pepper. Mix well.
- Heat until the cheese has melted and the pasta is creamy.
- Serve with grated cheese.

14. One Pot Chicken Pasta
(Prep time: 30 minutes. Calories: 500)
Ingredients
- 1 box pasta
- 1 tbsp olive oil
- 1 lb chicken cut into bite-sized pieces
- 1 tbsp all-purpose seasoning mix
- Salt and pepper
- 3 cloves garlic
- 1 can of sun-dried tomatoes, drained and chopped
- 1 ½ cups each of mozzarella cheese and whole milk
- ½ cup half and half
- ½ cup chicken broth
- 2 cups spinach leaves

Method
- Cook pasta according to instructions. Drain and set aside.
- In a skillet, add oil and put on medium heat.
- Sauté the chicken and season it. Cook until tender.
- Add the garlic and chopped sun-dried tomatoes.
- Add milk, broth, half and half and cheese. Cook until the sauce thickens.
- Add the pasta and spinach leaves. Cook until the leaves start to cook down. If the pasta seems dry, add some more water, milk or broth.

15. Easy Avocado Bean Salad

(Prep time: 20 minutes. Calories: 283)
Ingredients
• 2 large avocados, peeled, pitted and cubed
• ½ cup each chopped red bell pepper and green bell pepper
• 1 can of your choice of beans (pinto, red, etc.), washed and drained
• Large head of romaine lettuce
• For the dressing: ½ cup each olive oil and rice wine vinegar, 2 tsp each parsley and coriander, 2 tbsp honey, ½ tsp black pepper
Method
• Combine bell pepper, avocado and beans in a bowl.
• In another bowl, whisk together the dressing ingredients. Leave half of parsley for garnishing. Mix the bean mixture with the dressing to coat evenly.

• Arrange the salad over the lettuce leaves. Sprinkle leftover parsley to garnish. Serve immediately.

The dinner recipes included here typically take a maximum of 30 minutes to prepare, and all are nutritious and healthy. Enjoy!

1. Creamy Vegetable Fettuccine

(Prep time: 30 minutes. Calories: 312)

Ingredients

- 8 oz fettuccine pasta
- 1 cup each of sliced mushrooms, sliced red bell peppers, sliced green bell peppers, and broccoli florets
- 2 tsp olive oil
- 1 tsp butter.
- 1 tbsp all-purpose flour
- 2 cloves garlic crushed
- Parmesan cheese (to taste)
- 2 oz light cream cheese
- 2 oz crumbled gorgonzola cheese
- Salt and pepper
- 1 ¼ cups fat-free milk

Method

- Cook pasta according to directions.
- Steam all veggies until tender.
- In a large saucepan, heat the oil. Add crushed garlic. Let garlic brown. Then add flour and stir quickly. If desired, you can also add a teaspoon of butter.
- Add milk, cream cheese and gorgonzola cheeses. Stir and continue heating until the cheeses melt.
- Once sauce thickens, remove from heat. Now add the pasta and mix well. Add the vegetables and toss until mixed well.

• Top with grated parmesan and pepper.

2.Spinach and Sun-Dried Tomato Pizza

(Prep time: 25 minutes. Calories: 281 per slice)

Ingredients

- ½ cup dry packed sun-dried tomatoes
- 2 tbsp fresh basil
- 3 tbsp parmesan cheese
- ⅓ cup tomato juice
- 1 ready-to-use pizza dough base
- 1 tsp olive oil
- 2 cloves garlic
- 1 tbsp balsamic vinegar
- 2 tbsp tomato paste
- 2 cups fresh spinach leaves

Method

• Pour hot water on the sun-dried tomatoes and let them soak for 10 minutes.
• To prepare pesto: blend the tomatoes, tomato juice, tomato paste, basil, vinegar, olive oil, garlic and parmesan cheese.
• To assemble the pizza, spread the sauce on the pizza base. Top it with spinach leaves and sprinkle mozzarella on top.
• Bake according to directions until crust is cooked and cheese melts.

3.Greek Burgers

(Prep time: 20 minutes. Calories: 338)

Ingredients

- 1 lb ground beef
- 1 tsp oregano
- ¼ tsp black pepper
- 1 tbsp garlic
- 2 tbsp red onions, minced
- 1 oz crumbled feta cheese
- 4 whole wheat hamburger buns

Method

- Preheat grill.
- To make patties: combine the beef, spices, garlic, onions and form into 8 patties. Divide the cheese evenly over 4 of the patties. Top with remaining patties. Pinch the edges to seal.
- Grill the patties. Flip midway through cooking. Leave the patties on the heat for approximately 10-12 minutes. Do not overcook.
- Assemble the burger with tomato and cucumber slices.

4.Parmesan Garlic Salmon

(Prep time: 20 minutes. Calories: 318)

Ingredients

- 1 lb salmon
- 1 clove minced garlic
- ½ tsp Worcestershire sauce
- ⅓ cup mayonnaise
- 3 tbsp grated parmesan cheese
- 3 tbsp chopped onions or chives

Method

- Wash the fish fillets. Pat them dry.

• To make the sauce: mix garlic, Worcestershire sauce, mayo, onions and cheese.
• Spread the sauce evenly over the fish fillets. Place the fillet on a baking dish lined with butter paper.
• Bake for 15 minutes at 450 degrees.
• Serve with a side of steamed broccoli and other vegetables.

5.Black Bean and Corn Pita Pockets

(Prep time: 15 minutes. Calories: 430)

Ingredients

• 1 can low sodium black beans, drained and rinsed
• 1 cup frozen corn (thawed)
• 1 cup low sodium canned tomatoes or fresh chopped tomatoes
• 1 chopped avocado
• 1 tsp chopped parsley
• Salt and pepper to taste
• ⅓ cup shredded mozzarella
• 2 tsp lemon juice
• 1 tsp chili powder
• 4 pita pockets made with whole wheat

Method

• In a bowl, combine beans, corn, tomatoes, avocado, parsley, lemon juice, chili powder, salt and pepper.
• Cut pita bread in half to form pockets. Fill each pocket with the bean mixture. Add cheese and parsley on top. Serve.

6.Chicken Tortas

(Prep time: 15 minutes. Calories: 383)

Ingredients

- 2 cups of boiled and shredded chicken
- 1 tsp chili powder
- 2 cups fresh salsa
- 2 cups shredded lettuce
- 4 thin slices of white onions
- ½ cup grated cheese (feta or Monterey jack)
- 2 sliced radishes
- 1 avocado, chopped
- 1 large roll of French bread, cut in half

Method

- In a bowl, mix together the chicken, chili powder, and salsa.
- In another bowl, combine the vegetables (lettuce, onions, cheese and radishes).
- Evenly spoon the chicken and lettuce mixtures inside the bread. Top with fresh salsa and serve.

7. Healthy Gyro

(Prep time: 25 minutes. Calories: 500)

Gyros are a Greek dish made with rotisserie meat and served inside pita pockets.

Ingredients

- 1 cup sliced onion
- 2 cups each sliced green and red bell peppers
- 1 tbsp lemon juice
- 1 tbsp olive oil
- ½ lb turkey or chicken, cut in strips
- 1 medium apple, cored and sliced
- 6 whole wheat pita pockets
- ½ cup Greek low fat yogurt

Method

- In a skillet, heat oil. Add the onion, salt, lemon juice and bell peppers. Sauté until brown and crisp.
- Stir in the chicken or turkey and sauté until the meat is cooked.
- Remove from heat. Add the apple slices.
- Beat the yogurt with a fork until liquid.
- To assemble the gyro: add the apple-meat mixture to the pita and fold. Add the yogurt on top. Serve warm.

8.One Pot Turkey Dinner

(Prep time: 30 minutes. Calories: 286)

Ingredients

- ¾ lb ground turkey
- 1 medium onion, chopped
- 2 medium zucchinis, sliced
- 3 tomatoes, chopped
- 3 tbsp tomato paste
- Olive oil
- 1 tsp each oregano, thyme, basil and garlic powders
- Salt and pepper

Method

- In a pan, add olive oil and heat.
- Add the ground turkey and onions. Fry until onions are brown and soft, about 10 minutes.

- Add the remaining ingredients and simmer for 10 minutes.
- Add zucchini and cook for 5 minutes more.
- Serve with salad, white rice or brown rice.

9. Lemon Chicken with Herbs and Vegetables

(Prep time: 30 minutes. Calories: 400)

Ingredients

- ½ lb small red potatoes, cubed
- 1 ½ cups baby carrots
- 1 cup green beans, trimmed
- 2 boneless, skinless chicken breasts, halved
- 1 tbsp olive oil
- ½ cup lemon juice
- 2 tbsp honey
- 1 tbsp chopped fresh rosemary or 1 tsp dried rosemary
- 1 tsp lemon zest
- Salt and pepper to taste

Method

- Cook potatoes, carrots, and beans in boiling water for 8 minutes. Drain the water and set the veggies aside.
- In a medium skillet, heat olive oil and add the chicken breasts. Cook each breast for 3-4 minutes on either side.
- Add the boiled vegetables and remaining ingredients except lemon juice to the skillet. Cover and cook for 5 minutes.
- Turn off heat. Taste test and adjust seasonings to your preference. Add lemon juice and serve with a crisp green salad.

CONCLUSION

Some people don't realize the importance of diet and nutrition until they've already succumbed to an illness. Don't wait until you're already suffering from high blood pressure, high cholesterol or any other condition that puts your life in peril before you start thinking about what you eat.

If you want a diet that's good for your health and is relatively easy to stick to, the Mediterranean Diet program should be at the top of your list.

As you've found out from this book, the Mediterranean Diet has numerous health benefits, and most of these are backed by scientific research.

That's not all. It's also an effective tool for weight loss. If you want to slim down and look better, this is a great diet to consider. Not only it's safe and effective, but also provides long-term results.

Just make sure that you follow all the guidelines given in this book, and pair your healthy diet with regular exercise and healthy habits.

Printed in Great Britain
by Amazon

40216929R00086